VIRGINIA
SOCIAL Studies

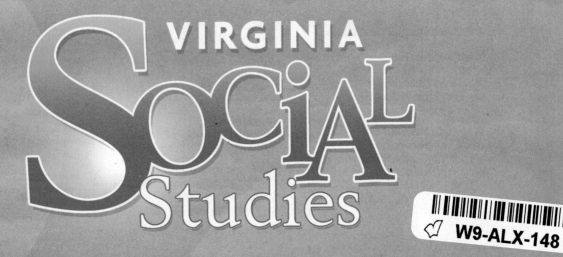

Exploring Your World, Past and Present

HOUGHTON MIFFLIN HARCOURT
School Publishers

Series Authors

Dr. Michael J. Berson
Professor
Social Science Education
University of South Florida
Tampa, Florida

Dr. Tyrone C. Howard
Associate Professor
UCLA Graduate School of Education &
   Information Studies
University of California Los Angeles
Los Angeles, California

Sara Shoob
Adjunct Instructor
George Mason University
Retired Social Studies Coordinator
Fairfax County Public Schools

Dr. Cinthia Salinas
Associate Professor
Department of Curriculum and
   Instruction
College of Education
The University of Texas at Austin
Austin, Texas

Virginia Consultants and Reviewers

Aliceyn S. Applewhite
Teacher
Park View Elementary School
Portsmouth, Virginia

Becky W. Baskerville
Principal
Sutherland Elementary School
Sutherland, Virginia

Deanna Beacham
Weapemeoc
Virginia Indian History Consultant
Mechanicsville, Virginia

Lauren W. Berents
Teacher
Shady Grove Elementary School
Glen Allen, Virginia

Katherine R. Bohn
Teacher
Glen Forest Elementary School
Falls Church, Virginia

Kim Briggs
Teacher
Leesville Road Elementary School
Lynchburg, Virginia

Susan K. Dalton
Teacher
Woodstock Elementary School
Virginia Beach, Virginia

James J. Doran
Teacher
Olive Branch Elementary School
Portsmouth, Virginia

Agnes Dunn
Retired Coordinator for Social Studies
Stafford County Public Schools

Jeanie Hawks
Instructional Technology Specialist
Halifax County Public Schools

Sarah Duncan Hinds
Social Studies Instructional Specialist
Portsmouth Public Schools
Portsmouth, Virginia

Carter H. McIntyre
Teacher
Laurel Meadow Elementary School
Mechanicsville, Virginia

Rebecca Mills
Supervisor of Social Studies
Spotsylvania County Public Schools

Jaime Ratliff
Teacher
Stonewall Elementary School
Clearbrook, Virginia

Tanya Lee Siwik
Teacher
Kings Park Elementary School
Springfield, Virginia

Evelyn Soltes
Title 1 Specialist for School
   Improvement
Richmond Public Schools
Richmond, Virginia

Andrea Nelson Tavenner
Teacher
Swift Creek Elementary School
Midlothian, Virginia

Kathryn Clawson Watkins
Retired Teacher
Chesterfield County

Cathy H. Whittecar
Teacher
Centerville Elementary School
Virginia Beach, Virginia

Karenne Wood
Monacan
Director
Virginia Indian Heritage Program
Kents Store, Virginia

ISBN-13: 978-0-15-384349-5
ISBN-10: 0-15-384349-7

10 11 1421 17 16 15
4500533279

Planet Friendly Publishing
Made in the United States
Printed on 100% Recycled Text Paper
By using this paper, each year we achieve the following environmental benefits from this title:

- Trees Saved: 71
- Greenhouse Gases Saved: 17,063 pounds
- Wastewater Saved: 13,662 gallons
- Solid Waste Saved: 5,012 pounds

- *Learn more about our Planet Friendly Publishing efforts at greenedition.org*

- *Environmental impact estimates calculated using the Environmental Paper Network's Paper Calculator. For more information, visit http://calculator.environmentalpaper.org.*

Using Your Interactive Textbook

Dear _____

This year you will be using a different kind of textbook. What makes it different? You can write in it! It's **interactive**.

TextWork

As you read each lesson, look for the green TextWork boxes. Each box has numbered questions and activities for you to complete. You'll be asked to underline, circle, and draw in your book. And you can write the answers right below the questions! So keep those pencils sharp and markers ready.

Explore!

Sometimes you'll see this symbol in your book. It tells you that you or your teacher can explore something in greater detail. You might study an object more closely, take a virtual tour of a place, or watch a video about an important event. These are just a few of the ways that you can explore more online with Electronic Interactive Presentations (EIP).

Are you ready to use a new kind of textbook? Then let's get started!

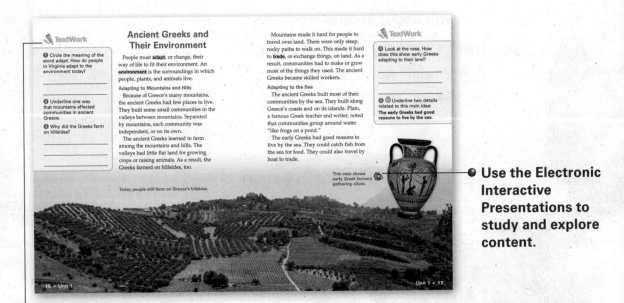

• **Use the words and illustrations to complete the TextWork.**

• **Use the Electronic Interactive Presentations to study and explore content.**

iv

Unit 2

Ancient Rome

History 3.1; Geography 3.4; Economics 3.7

v

Unit 5

The World Around Us

Looking at Earth

Globes and maps help people study Earth. A **globe** is a model of Earth. It shows Earth's round shape.

A **map** is a flat drawing of a place on Earth. Looking at a map of a place is like seeing it from an airplane. A map shows an aerial (AIR•ee•uhl) view of a place. An **aerial view** is the view from above.

MacArthur Center

Battleship Wisconsin

Maps can show more details, or information, about a place than a globe can. A map can show the whole Earth or just a small part of it. Maps use colors, drawings, and symbols to show details. The map below shows some details of Norfolk, Virginia. You can see these details in the aerial view of the city.

Berkley Bridge

Waterside Festival Marketplace

Town Point Park

Norfolk, Virginia

Brambleton Avenue

St. Pauls Boulevard

MacArthur Center

Wells Theatre

City Hall Avenue

Boush Street

Norfolk

Waterside Drive

264

Berkley Bridge

Norfolk

Waterside Festival Marketplace

Pagoda Park

Town Point Park

Battleship Wisconsin

Elizabeth River

Map Legend
■ Point of interest

0   500   1,000 Feet

0   150   300 Meters

Land and Water

You can use a globe or a map to locate, or find, Earth's land and water features. Because of its round shape, a globe can only show one half of Earth at a time. On a world map, you can see all of the land and water at one time.

Earth's largest areas of land are called **continents**. Earth has seven continents. You can see each of these continents on the map below.

Earth's largest bodies of water are called **oceans**. Earth has five oceans. You can also see each of these oceans on the map below.

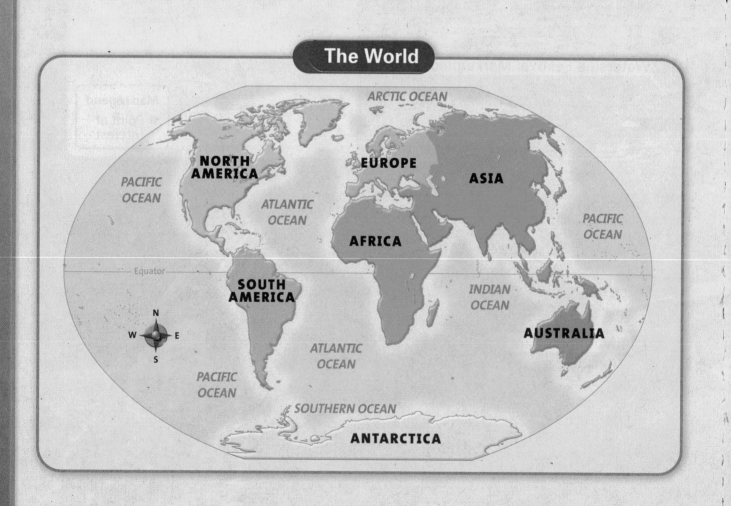

The World

The Equator

The **equator** is an imaginary line around the middle of Earth. The equator divides Earth into two equal halves, or **hemispheres**. The Northern Hemisphere is north of the equator. The Southern Hemisphere is south of it.

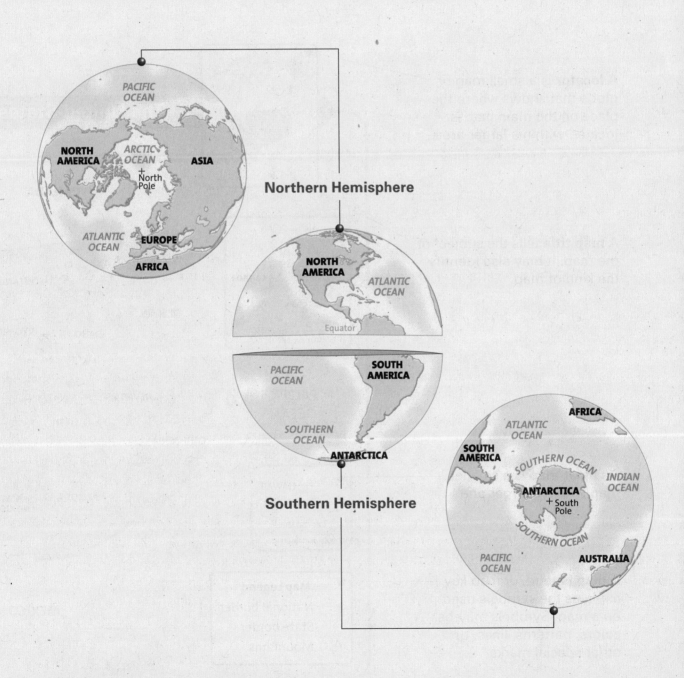

Northern Hemisphere

Southern Hemisphere

Reading Maps

Maps give different kinds of information about Earth and the world around you. To help you read maps more easily, mapmakers add certain features to most maps they draw. These features usually include a title, a map legend, and a compass rose.

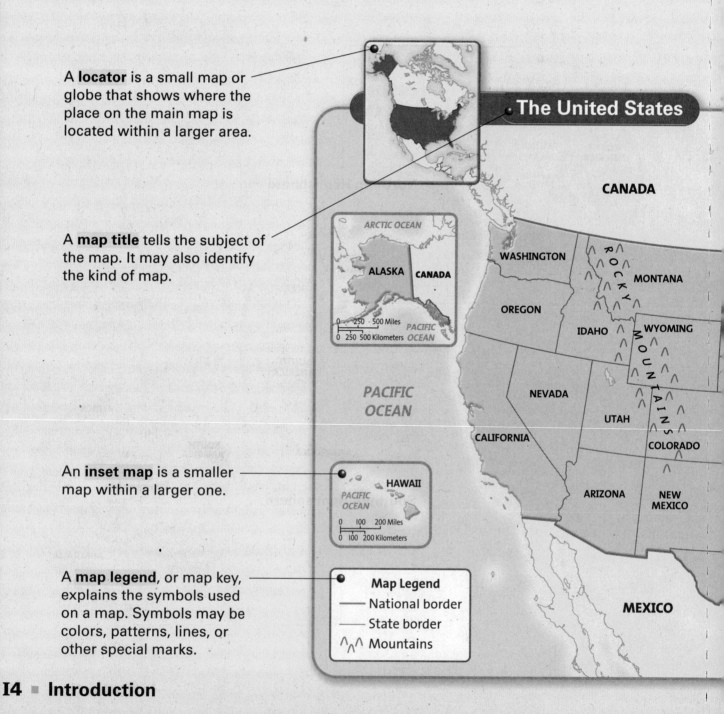

A **locator** is a small map or globe that shows where the place on the main map is located within a larger area.

A **map title** tells the subject of the map. It may also identify the kind of map.

An **inset map** is a smaller map within a larger one.

A **map legend**, or map key, explains the symbols used on a map. Symbols may be colors, patterns, lines, or other special marks.

The United States

CANADA

ARCTIC OCEAN

ALASKA CANADA

0 250 500 Miles
0 250 500 Kilometers

PACIFIC OCEAN

PACIFIC OCEAN

WASHINGTON

OREGON

IDAHO

NEVADA

CALIFORNIA

UTAH

ARIZONA

MONTANA

WYOMING

COLORADO

NEW MEXICO

ROCKY MOUNTAINS

HAWAII

PACIFIC OCEAN

0 100 200 Miles
0 100 200 Kilometers

MEXICO

Map Legend
— National border
— State border
∧∧∧ Mountains

Mapmakers sometimes need to show places marked on a map in greater detail or places that are located beyond the area shown on the map. Find Alaska and Hawaii on the map below. To show this much detail for these states and the rest of the country, the map would have to be much larger. Instead, Alaska and Hawaii are each shown as a separate inset map, or a smaller map within a larger map.

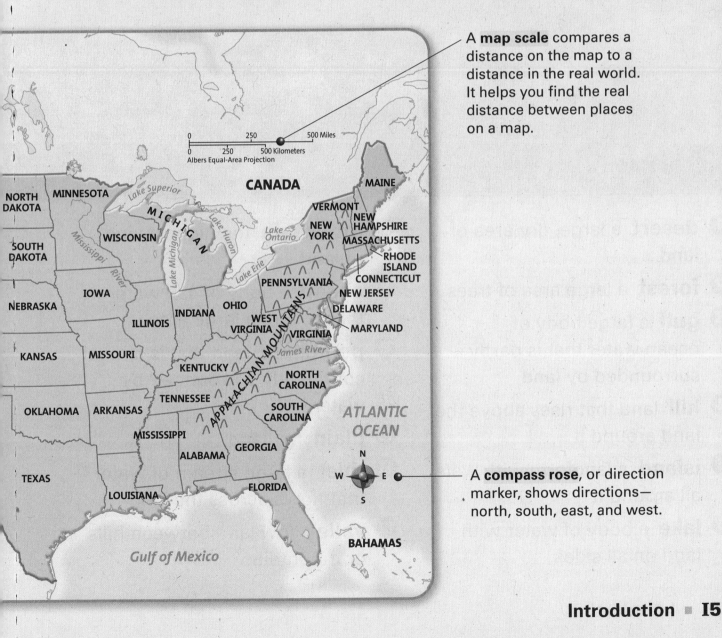

A **map scale** compares a distance on the map to a distance in the real world. It helps you find the real distance between places on a map.

A **compass rose**, or direction marker, shows directions—north, south, east, and west.

Geography Terms

① **desert** a large, dry area of land

② **forest** a large area of trees

③ **gulf** a large body of ocean water that is partly surrounded by land

④ **hill** land that rises above the land around it

⑤ **island** a landform with water all around it

⑥ **lake** a body of water with land on all sides

⑦ **mountain** the highest kind of land

⑧ **ocean** a body of salt water that covers a large area

⑨ **peninsula** land that is almost completely surrounded by water

⑩ **plain** flat land

⑪ **river** a large stream of water that flows across the land

⑫ **valley** low land between hills or mountains

Ancient Greece

The Parthenon sits on a
hilltop in Athens, Greece.

Spotlight on Standards

THE BIG IDEA Over time, people find new
ways of living and doing things. They share
these new ideas with others.

HISTORY AND SOCIAL SCIENCE SOL
3.1, 3.4a, 3.4b, 3.4c, 3.7

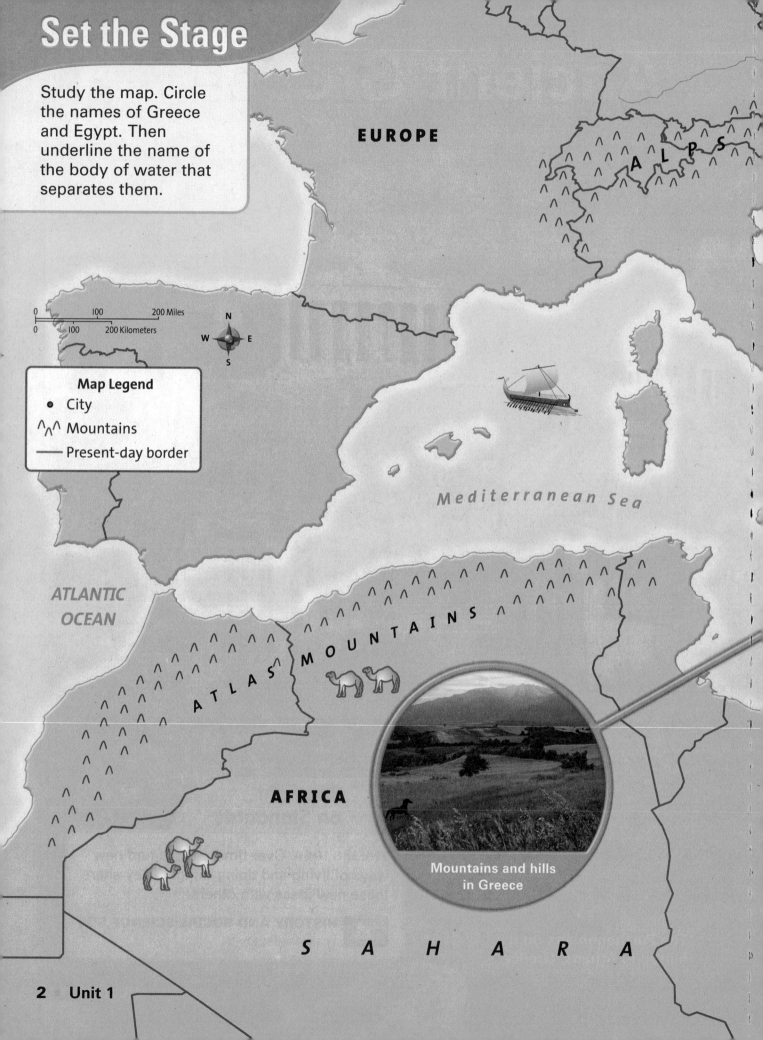

Set the Stage

Study the map. Circle the names of Greece and Egypt. Then underline the name of the body of water that separates them.

EUROPE

ALPS

Map Legend
- City
- ^^^ Mountains
- —— Present-day border

0   100   200 Miles
0   100   200 Kilometers

N
W   E
S

Mediterranean Sea

ATLANTIC
OCEAN

ATLAS MOUNTAINS

AFRICA

Mountains and hills
in Greece

S A H A R A

The Lands Around Ancient Greece

EUROPE

ASIA

The Parthenon of ancient Greece

Aegean Sea

GREECE

Athens

Mediterranean Sea

The pyramids of ancient Egypt

Cairo

EGYPT

Nile River

Red Sea

AFRICA

Set the Stage

1 Why do you think parts of this building have lasted so long?

_____

_____

2 How do you know that sports were important to the people of ancient Greece? Underline the words that tell why.

A Family in Ancient Greece
Members of a Greek family had different roles.

Parts of this building from ancient Greece still stand.

Greek Athletes
Competed in the first Olympic Games more than 2,300 years ago

Pericles
A Greek leader who helped make Athens a great city

Preview Vocabulary

characteristic

Characteristics are different traits. Greece's characteristics make it special. p. 12

natural resource

The Greeks used **natural resources**, or materials that come from nature, to grow crops. p. 21

human resource

The Greeks used **human resources**, or workers, to build beautiful statues and buildings. p. 21

capital resource

The Greeks used **capital resources** to make goods. Tools are one kind of capital resource. p. 21

contribution

The Olympic Games are a contribution from ancient Greece. A **contribution** is an act of giving. p. 28

direct democracy

The government of ancient Greece was a **direct democracy**. People voted to make their own laws. p. 31

Reading Social Studies

⭐ Focus Skill — Main Idea and Details

Learn

The **main idea** is the most important idea of a paragraph. The main idea is often in the first sentence. **Details** give more information about the main idea.

Main Idea

The most important idea

⬆

Details

| Fact about the main idea | Fact about the main idea | Fact about the main idea |

Practice

Read the paragraphs. Circle the main idea. Then underline the details. The first paragraph has been done for you.

(Long ago, the Egyptians, the Greeks, and other people lived along the Mediterranean (meh•duh•tuh•RAY•nee•uhn) Sea.) **Main Idea**

These different groups of people all used the sea as a way to travel. **Details**

Travel allowed people to trade, or exchange, things. They shared goods and ideas with each other. Today, the Mediterranean Sea is still important to many groups of people.

Read the following paragraphs. Then complete the activities below.

The Mediterranean Sea

The Mediterranean Sea is the third-largest sea in the world. Its deep blue waters cover a huge area. The sea stretches about 2,500 miles from east to west. It is about 500 miles wide from north to south.

The Mediterranean Sea is almost completely surrounded by land. In fact, *mediterranean* is a Latin word that means "in the middle of land." Europe lies to the north and west of the Mediterranean Sea. Africa is to the south of the sea, and Asia is to the east of it.

The Mediterranean Sea is really a part of the much larger Atlantic Ocean. The two bodies of water are separated only by a narrow body of water. This narrow body of water is called the Strait of Gibraltar (juh•BRAWL•ter).

The Strait of Gibraltar is only about 8 miles wide. It lies between steep rock cliffs and separates Europe from Africa.

1. **In the first paragraph, circle the main idea and underline the details.**

2. **What is the main idea of the second paragraph?**

   _____

   _____

3. **In the last paragraph, underline the details that give information about the Strait of Gibraltar.**

Greece's Location and Land

In **ancient** times, or times very long ago, many people settled on land near the Mediterranean Sea. Among these people were the ancient Greeks. They lived on land in what is now the country of Greece. **Think about the land where the ancient Greeks settled.**

The sea was important to the ancient Greeks.

Essential Questions
✓ Where was ancient Greece located?
✓ What were the physical characteristics of ancient Greece?

SOL **HISTORY AND SOCIAL SCIENCE SOL**
3.4a, 3.4b

**TextWork**

❶ List two details about the location of ancient Greece.

near the mediterraneans Greece is in southern Europe

❷ Study the globe and map on page 11. On the globe, circle the name of the continent where Greece is located. On the map, underline the name of the sea that surrounds Greece.

The Location of Ancient Greece

Long ago, the ancient Egyptians farmed along the Nile River in Africa, near the Mediterranean Sea. As time passed, the Egyptians built large cities and pyramids.

At about the same time, the ancient Greeks were settling land across the Mediterranean Sea. Their land was a place of mountains and mostly dry, rocky soil.

Settling Along the Mediterranean Sea

Ancient Greece was located on land near the Mediterranean Sea. This land is now the country of Greece. Greece is in southern Europe.

The Greeks built the Temple of Poseidon (puh•SY•duhn) to honor their god of the sea.

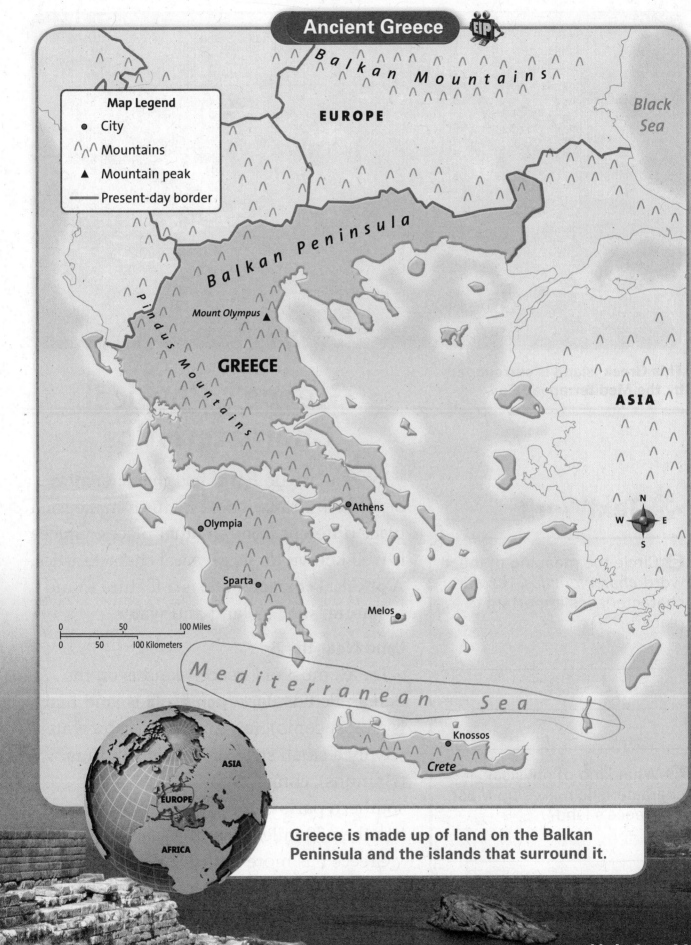

Ancient Greece

Map Legend
- City
- ∧∧∧ Mountains
- ▲ Mountain peak
- —— Present-day border

Balkan Mountains

EUROPE

Black Sea

Balkan Peninsula

Pindus Mountains

Mount Olympus ▲

GREECE

ASIA

Athens

Olympia

N
W E
S

Sparta

Melos

| 0 | 50 | 100 Miles |
| 0 | 50 | 100 Kilometers |

Mediterranean Sea

Knossos

Crete

ASIA

EUROPE

AFRICA

Greece is made up of land on the Balkan Peninsula and the islands that surround it.

This Greek island is surrounded by the Mediterranean Sea.

TextWork

3 Circle the meaning of the word *characteristics*. How are characteristics important to a place?

_____

_____

_____

4 What kind of physical characteristic makes up most of Greece's land?

_____

Greece's Physical Characteristics

Every place on Earth has **characteristics**, or different traits. These features make each place different from all other places. Greece is well known for its physical characteristics. A **physical characteristic** is a feature found in nature, such as land and water.

Land Near the Sea

Today, most of Greece's land is on the Balkan Peninsula. A **peninsula** is land that is almost completely surrounded by water. Only a small strip of land, or isthmus (IS•muhs), connects the northern and southern parts of Greece. Most of Greece is less than 50 miles from the sea.

Greece has more than 2,000 islands surrounding its coast. Most are small, with villages dotting their coasts.

Mountains, Hills, and Valleys

Mountains stretch across much of Greece. Between the mountains are low hills and narrow valleys. In ancient Greece, people first started their communities in these areas. A **community** is a place where people live, work, and play. The mountains often divided communities from one another.

The ancient Greeks had few good places for farming. There is a limited amount of rich soil. The soil in the mountains is thin and rocky. The best soil is in the valleys.

Mountains also affect Greece's climate. **Climate** is the weather that a place has over a long period of time. Mountains give Greece a mild, dry climate. It is often warm, and there is not a lot of rain.

TextWork

5 (Focus Skill) What is the main idea of the second paragraph?

_____

_____

_____

_____

6 Scan, or quickly look over, the text on this page. Underline the sentence that explains why Greece has a limited amount of rich soil.

Mount Olympus is the highest mountain in Greece.

1. **SUMMARIZE** Where was ancient Greece located?

_____

_____

_____

_____

2. What are three examples of **physical characteristics**?

_____

_____

_____

Circle the letter of the correct answer.

3. Which BEST describes ancient Greece's land?

   A Fertile soil, cold climate, islands

   B A peninsula, islands, mountains

   C Flat land, fertile soil, hills

   D Islands, lots of rain, mountains

4. Greece has few good places for farming because—

   F rich soil is limited

   G the land has many islands

   H the rocks are thin

   J the climate is too rainy

Draw a line connecting each physical characteristic of Greece on the left with the correct description on the right.

5. valleys   makes up most of Greece's land

6. isthmus   have the best soil for farming

7. peninsula   connects the northern and southern parts of Greece

writing

Write a Booklet Create a booklet about ancient Greece. Write about its land and location. Then draw pictures and maps to illustrate your booklet.

Greece

This globe shows Greece's location.

Using Greece's Land

The places where people live often affect how they live. The mountains and the Mediterranean Sea affected the lives of the ancient Greeks. **Think about how Greece's land and location affected how the ancient Greeks lived.**

This town in Greece was built between the mountains and the sea.

Essential Questions

✓ What were the physical characteristics of ancient Greece?

✓ How did the people of ancient Greece adapt to and change their environment to meet their needs?

HISTORY AND SOCIAL SCIENCE SOL
3.4b, 3.4c

Ancient Greeks and Their Environment

❶ Circle the meaning of the word *adapt*. How do people in Virginia adapt to the environment today?

_____

_____

❷ Underline one way that mountains affected communities in ancient Greece.

❸ Why did the Greeks farm on hillsides?

_____

_____

_____

People must **adapt**, or change, their way of life to fit their environment. An **environment** is the surroundings in which people, plants, and animals live.

Adapting to Mountains and Hills

Because of Greece's many mountains, the ancient Greeks had few places to live. They built some small communities in the valleys between mountains. Separated by mountains, each community was independent, or on its own.

The ancient Greeks learned to farm among the mountains and hills. The valleys had little flat land for growing crops or raising animals. As a result, the Greeks farmed on hillsides, too.

Today people still farm on Greece's hillsides.

Mountains made it hard for people to travel over land. There were only steep, rocky paths to walk on. This made it hard to **trade**, or exchange things, on land. As a result, communities had to make or grow most of the things they used. The ancient Greeks became skilled workers.

Adapting to the Sea

The ancient Greeks built most of their communities by the sea. They built along Greece's coasts and on its islands. Plato, a famous Greek teacher and writer, noted that communities group around water "like frogs on a pond."

The early Greeks had good reasons to live by the sea. They could catch fish from the sea for food. They could also travel by boat to trade.

This vase shows early Greek farmers gathering olives.

TextWork

4 Look at the vase. How does this show early Greeks adapting to their land?

_____

_____

_____

5 (Focus Skill) Underline two details related to this main idea: **The early Greeks had good reasons to live by the sea.**

1. **SUMMARIZE** How did the ancient Greeks adapt to their environment?

_____

_____

_____

2. Use the word **trade** in a sentence about ancient Greece.

_____

_____

_____

_____

Circle the letter of the correct answer.

3. The ancient Greeks farmed on hillsides—

   A because the soil was best there

   B to avoid flooding rivers

   C because the valleys had little flat land for farming

   D to get more sun for their crops

4. Where did the ancient Greeks build most of their communities?

   F By the sea

   G On hillsides

   H On mountains

   J In valleys between mountains

Draw a line connecting each word on the left with the correct definition on the right.

5. environment   to change

6. adapt   to exchange things

7. trade   surroundings   This trade item shows an early Greek farmer.

writing

Make a List List ways that the ancient Greeks adapted to their environment. Give your list a title, and number each item.

Living in Ancient Greece

The ancient Greeks used different kinds of resources to get or make the things they used every day. Greek workers used resources to do different kinds of jobs. **Think about how the ancient Greeks may have used resources to make things and to do things for people.**

Many cities in ancient Greece had an open-air market.

Essential Questions

✓ What were the human characteristics of ancient Greece?
✓ How do producers use natural, human, and capital resources to produce goods and services?
✓ What are some of the goods and services produced in ancient Greece?
✓ What resources (natural, human, capital) were used to produce goods and services in ancient Greece?

HISTORY AND SOCIAL SCIENCE SOL
3.4b, 3.7

1 ⭐Focus Skill Underline the main idea of the first paragraph.

2 Circle three examples of goods made in ancient Greece. Draw a box around two examples of services in ancient Greece.

3 Use the word *producer* in a sentence.

_____

_____

_____

_____

Goods and Services

A **good** is something that people make or use to satisfy needs and wants. Goods in ancient Greece included crops and ships. The Greeks also made pottery, or vases, bowls, and other items made from clay.

Other workers provided services. A **service** is work that someone does for someone else. Some ancient Greeks worked as traders to help people get goods. Others were soldiers who helped protect their community.

People who use resources to make goods or provide services are called **producers**. A resource is something that people use to meet their needs and wants. The kinds of goods and services a producer makes depend on the resources available.

Using Resources

Producers use three kinds of resources to produce goods and services. **Natural resources** are materials that come from nature. The Greeks used water and soil to raise crops and used wood to build ships.

Producers in ancient Greece also needed human resources. **Human resources** are workers who produce goods or services. In ancient Greece, farming and shipbuilding needed many workers.

Producers also used **capital resources**, or goods made by people and used to produce other goods and services. Capital resources include machines, tools, and buildings. Farmers and shipbuilders in ancient Greece used tools in their work.

4 List the three kinds of resources.

_____

_____

_____

_____

5 Study the illustration. Label each kind of resource shown.

Greek Shipbuilding

The Greeks used different resources to build ships.

_____

Today, people in Greece still farm on terraces.

Human Characteristics

Besides physical characteristics, most environments have **human characteristics**. These are features made by people. Human characteristics include cities, farms, roads, and ways of life, such as jobs.

Farmers

The ancient Greeks lived among mountains with limited rich soil. Farmers made more flat land for raising crops by building terraces. A **terrace** is a flat area dug into the side of a hill or mountain.

Farmers chose crops that grow well in Greece's soil. They planted wheat, grapes, and olives. They also chose animals that need only small areas for grazing. They raised sheep, goats, and pigs on hillsides.

TextWork

6 Skim the headings on pages 22–23. Circle the three kinds of workers that were important to the ancient Greeks.

7 Why is a terrace a human characteristic?

_____

_____

8 What are examples of crops grown in Greece?

_____

_____

Shipbuilders

The ancient Greeks used wood from forests to build ships. They used their ships to fish, to travel among the Greek islands, and to sail the Mediterranean Sea. Fishers caught tuna, shellfish, squid, and octopus with spears and nets. The Greeks then sold these goods in markets.

An ancient Greek cup

Traders

Through sea travel, the Greeks stayed connected. They used ships to trade with one another and with other people living along the Mediterranean Sea. Trade allowed the Greeks to get goods they did not have or could not make themselves. For example, the Greeks traded olive oil, pottery, leather, and wood for iron, gold, and ivory. Trade also allowed the Greeks to exchange ideas with other people.

TextWork

9 How was trading connected to shipbuilding in ancient Greece?

_____

_____

10 Underline the reasons why trade was important to the ancient Greeks.

Greek traders unload their ships at a port.

Life in Athens

Some Greek communities grew rich from trade. They began to grow into cities. Some cities became parts of larger communities called city-states. Each city-state connected a city to the farms, towns, and villages around it. Athens was one of the most important Greek city-states.

The City of Athens

Athens was similar to other Greek city-states. Most Greek city-states had an acropolis (uh•KRAH•puh•luhs). This fort was built on top of a hill to protect the city. Later, it became a center of religion.

Around the acropolis, the Greeks built houses, temples, and an agora (A•guh•ruh). An agora was an outdoor market and a meeting place. The Greeks visited the agora to trade goods and talk about the news.

TextWork

11 Read the first paragraph on this page. Underline the human characteristics of a city-state.

12 How does an acropolis have both physical and human characteristics?

_____

_____

_____

_____

Greeks visited the agora in Athens to trade goods.

The agora was the center of Greek life. In workshops, craftworkers made products to sell. They made pottery, leather goods, and metal goods. At stalls, people sold fruits and vegetables from nearby farms. Traders sold goods from other parts of the world.

Education and Work

Workers in Athens learned their jobs in different ways. Most boys went to school. They studied math, reading, and writing. At 14, they learned their father's job by becoming potters, carpenters, and metalworkers. Girls studied math, reading, and writing at home. They also learned other skills. Their mothers taught them how to cook, sew, and take care of children.

TextWork

13 How did most Athenian children learn their jobs and skills?

_____

_____

_____

_____

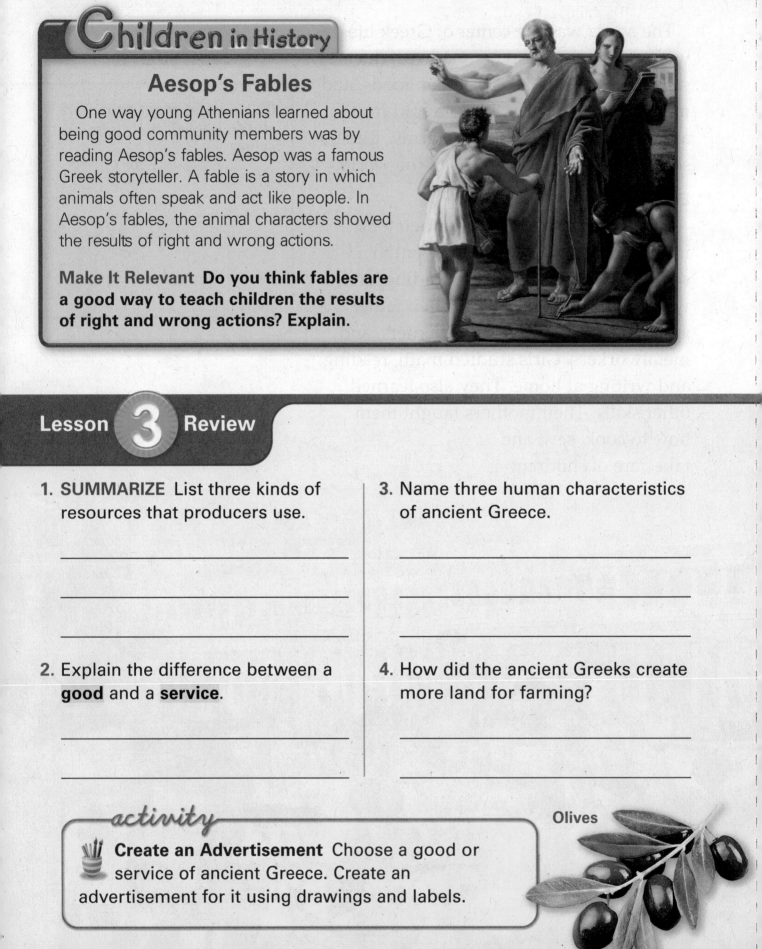

Children in History

Aesop's Fables

One way young Athenians learned about being good community members was by reading Aesop's fables. Aesop was a famous Greek storyteller. A fable is a story in which animals often speak and act like people. In Aesop's fables, the animal characters showed the results of right and wrong actions.

Make It Relevant Do you think fables are a good way to teach children the results of right and wrong actions? Explain.

Lesson 3 Review

1. **SUMMARIZE** List three kinds of resources that producers use.

_____

_____

_____

2. Explain the difference between a **good** and a **service**.

_____

_____

3. Name three human characteristics of ancient Greece.

_____

_____

_____

4. How did the ancient Greeks create more land for farming?

_____

_____

activity

Create an Advertisement Choose a good or service of ancient Greece. Create an advertisement for it using drawings and labels.

Olives

Contributions of Ancient Greece

In time, ancient Greece grew into a great civilization. A **civilization** is a large group of people living in an organized way. The ancient Greek civilization started new ideas. Many of these ideas are still important today. **Think about how the ideas of the ancient Greeks are still important today.**

The Parthenon in Athens, Greece

Essential Questions
- What styles in architecture used today came from ancient Greece?
- What principles of government from ancient Greece are part of our government?
- What sporting events today came from ancient Greece?

HISTORY AND SOCIAL SCIENCE SOL
3.1

Gifts from Greece

The ancient Greeks made important contributions that still influence the lives of people today. A **contribution** is an act of giving or doing something that improves a situation.

The ancient Greeks came up with many new ideas. They found better ways to run their government. A **government** is a group of people that makes laws for a community, a state, or a country.

The ancient Greeks made important contributions in other ways, too. They created new styles of building, or **architecture** (AR•kuh•tek•cher). They thought of new forms of art and ways of learning. They celebrated competition in sports.

Greek Columns

Doric   Ionic   Corinthian

The ancient Greeks used three different styles of columns.

TextWork

1 (Focus Skill) Circle the main idea of the first paragraph.

2 Scan this page. Underline five kinds of contributions made by the ancient Greeks.

The Parthenon, in Athens, is an example of how the ancient Greeks used columns.

Architecture

The people of Athens took great pride in the beauty of their city. Architects designed new buildings that used white stone from nearby mountains. The architects also used stone columns in the construction of many of their buildings. A **column** is a support for a building's roof.

The Parthenon (PAR•thuh•nahn) is a good example of Greek architecture. This temple was built about 2,500 years ago. It had 64 columns. Part of this building still stands in Athens today.

Many buildings today use Greek designs and columns. One example is the Virginia Capitol in Richmond. Another is the United States Supreme Court building in Washington, D.C.

TextWork

❸ How were columns important to Greek architecture?

A column is a support for a building's roof

❹ Underline the sentence that explains why Greek contributions to architecture are important.

Virginia Capitol

The ancient Greeks performed plays in theaters.

A Greek mosaic

The Arts and Learning

Art was an important part of the buildings of ancient Greece. Greek artists decorated buildings with paintings, sculptures, and mosaics. A **mosaic** is a picture made from small pieces of glass or stone. Art often showed scenes from daily life or Greek stories.

Greek writers wrote many plays. The plays were performed in theaters and at Greek festivals. They also wrote poetry and wrote about their history. People today still read the words of Greek writers.

Learning grew in ancient Greece as well. Many great thinkers and teachers lived in Athens. Socrates (SAH•kruh•teez) and Plato were two important Greek teachers.

The First Democracy

Athens started the world's first democracy. In a **democracy**, the citizens make the decisions by voting. Greece is often called the birthplace of democracy.

All free men could take part in Athens's democracy. They met in a group called an assembly. They voted to make their own rules and laws. This kind of government is called a **direct democracy**.

Decisions were made by **majority rule**. Every member had one vote. The idea that received the majority of the votes, or more than half of the votes, passed.

Today, many governments are based on the democratic ideas of the ancient Greeks. The governments of Virginia and of the United States are two examples.

TextWork

7 What kind of government did the people of Athens start?

Democracy

8 Underline the characteristics of a democracy.

9 Circle two governments that are based on the democratic ideas of Athens.

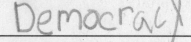

Biography

Trustworthiness

Pericles 🅴🅸🅿

Pericles (PAIR•uh•kleez) led Athens for 40 years because its citizens trusted him. While he was its leader, Athens grew to be a great city-state. Pericles had architects design many new buildings. One building was the Parthenon. Pericles also hired artists to create mosaics, sculptures, and paintings. He hired writers to tell Athens's history, too. This time in ancient Greece is known as the Golden Age of Athens.

Sports

The ancient Greeks never joined to form a single country. They each belonged to their own city-state. However, they did share the same beliefs. The ancient Greeks believed in many gods. They honored these gods in religious festivals.

10 What beliefs did the Greeks share?

_____

_____

11 How did the Olympic Games start?

_____

_____

_____

_____

12 Underline the sports that were part of the Olympic Games long ago.

One festival honored the Greek god Zeus. The festival was held every four years in Olympia. Athletes from the city-states competed in the Olympic Games.

The first Olympic Games took place more than 2,500 years ago. At that time, athletes competed only in footraces. Over time, other sports were added. They included the long jump, wrestling, boxing, chariot racing, and horse racing. Many sporting events of ancient Greece are still part of the Olympics Games today.

Runners competed in the 2008 Olympic Games in Beijing, China.

1. **SUMMARIZE** How have the ancient Greeks influenced the lives of people today?

_____

_____

_____

2. Write a sentence describing a **contribution** that ancient Greeks made to our way of life.

_____

_____

_____

3. What building of today was influenced by Greek architecture?

_____

_____

Circle the letter of the correct answer.

4. Which BEST describes the government of Athens?

   A The ruler decided everything.

   B All free men could take part in government by voting.

   C Everyone could take part in government.

   D A king made all the decisions.

Draw a line connecting each word on the left with the correct definition on the right.

5. democracy   The idea with the most votes passes.

6. direct democracy   Citizens make decisions by voting.

7. majority rule   All citizens vote to make their laws.

An Olympic gold medal

---

activity

🖌 **Make a Model** Make a model that shows one contribution from ancient Greece. Explain how the contribution affected life then and today.

Fun With Social Studies

Factory Fun
abc VOCABULARY

Match each word with a number at the Greek pottery factory. One is done for you.

- [ ] good
- [5] service
- [ ] natural resource
- [ ] human resource
- [ ] capital resource

Where in Greece?

Name the place in Greece that each person is describing.

This place is really part of the Atlantic Ocean.

The ruins of the Parthenon are here.

Ancient Greek athletes first competed here.

_____ _____ _____

Museum Mix-Up

Circle the two items that do not belong in the ancient Greek museum.

Pyramids

Mosaic

Great Wall

Sculpture

Column

Pottery

Review and Test Prep

The Big Idea

Over time, people find new ways of living and doing things. They share these new ideas with others.

Summarize the Unit

(Focus Skill) **Main Idea and Details** Complete the graphic organizer to show that you understand important ideas and details about ancient Greece.

Main Idea

The ancient Greeks made important contributions in architecture, government, and sports.

Details

_____ _____ _____

Use Vocabulary

Complete each sentence with a vocabulary term from the Word Bank.

1. The Olympic Games are a Greek _____.

2. Tools used to make products are _____.

3. Greece's _____ make it different from other places.

4. Water and soil are examples of _____.

Word Bank

characteristics
p. 12

natural resources
p. 21

human resources
p. 21

capital resources
p. 21

contribution
p. 28

Think About It

Circle the letter of the correct answer.

5.

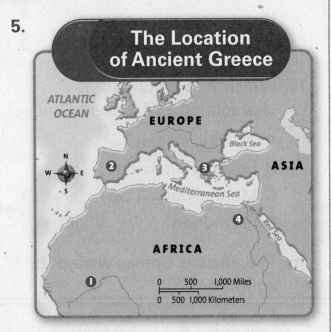

The Location of Ancient Greece

ATLANTIC OCEAN
EUROPE
Black Sea
❷
❸
ASIA
Mediterranean Sea
❹
Red Sea
AFRICA
❶

0   500   1,000 Miles
0   500 1,000 Kilometers

Which number shows where ancient Greece was located?

A 1

B 2

C 3

D 4

6. Which body of water was close to ancient Greece?

F Atlantic Ocean

G Mediterranean Sea

H Nile River

J Red Sea

7. Ancient Greece was located in—

A North America

B Asia

C Africa

D Europe

8.

- island
- mountain
- river

These are examples of—

F human characteristics

G human resources

H physical characteristics

J capital resources

9. The ancient Greeks adapted to an environment that included—

A seas and mountains

B many deserts and savannas

C many rivers and plains

D mountains and deserts

10. In ancient Greece, sailors, traders, and soldiers all provided—

F products

G services

H goods

J needs

11.

Alexander makes vases, bowls, and other items from clay. These goods are forms of pottery.

Alexander is an example of a—

A capital resource

B natural resource

C service

D producer

12.

The wood that ancient Greeks used to build ships is an example of a—

F mosaic

G natural resource

H service

J capital resource

13.

Main Idea

The ancient Greeks used three kinds of resources to farm.

Details

| Soil and water | Farmers | ? |

Which capital resource replaces the question mark?

A Producer

B Farmworkers

C Tools

D Service

14. The ancient Greeks changed their environment by—

F building terraces

G starting the Olympic Games

H creating democracy

J inventing columns

15. Which was a human characteristic of ancient Greece?

A Atlantic Ocean

B Balkan Peninsula

C Mediterranean Sea

D Parthenon

16. The ancient Greeks visited the agora to—

F study architecture

G trade goods

H raise crops

J build ships

17.

Which characteristic of the Parthenon did ancient Greek architects often use in buildings?

A Arches

B Large windows

C Columns

D Flat roofs

18.

- Doric
- Ionic
- Corinthian

These are examples of Greek—

F mosaics

G columns

H statues

J paintings

19. Greece's government was a—

A representative democracy

B dictatorship

C direct democracy

D monarchy

20.

- Direct Democracy
- The Columns of the Parthenon
- Mosaics, Sculptures, and Paintings
- The Olympic Games

Which of these should be the title of this list?

F Contributions of Ancient Greece

G Jobs of Ancient Greece

H Government of Ancient Greece

J The Arts of Ancient Greece

Answer these questions.

21. How was ancient Greece affected by its location on the Mediterranean Sea?

_____

_____

22. Explain how ancient Greek shipbuilders used natural resources, human resources, and capital resources.

_____

_____

_____

23. Which contributions of ancient Greece still affect life today? Why are these contributions important?

_____

_____

_____

An important statue has been stolen from a temple in ancient Greece! You and Eco have been asked to help solve the crime, but you'll need to use everything you know about ancient Greece to catch the thief. Go online to play the game now.

HMH

ECO

Show What You Know

✎ Writing Write an Article

Write an article telling how the contributions of ancient Greece affect our lives today. Include details about Greek ideas in our architecture, government, and sports. Find and use information from print and non-print sources in your article.

🖌 Activity Make a Museum

Make a museum exhibit about life in ancient Greece. List information to include about Greece's location, jobs, arts, sports, and government. Then prepare maps, drawings, models, and other items for your museum. Display these items on a table or bulletin board in your classroom. Invite other classes to visit your museum.

Ancient Rome

Ruins of the Roman
Forum in Rome, Italy

Spotlight on Standards

THE BIG IDEA The people of the past made contributions that influence the present.

SOL **HISTORY AND SOCIAL SCIENCE SOL**
3.1, 3.4a, 3.4b, 3.4c, 3.7

Set the Stage

Study the map. Circle Athens and Rome. Underline the name of the large body of water near both places.

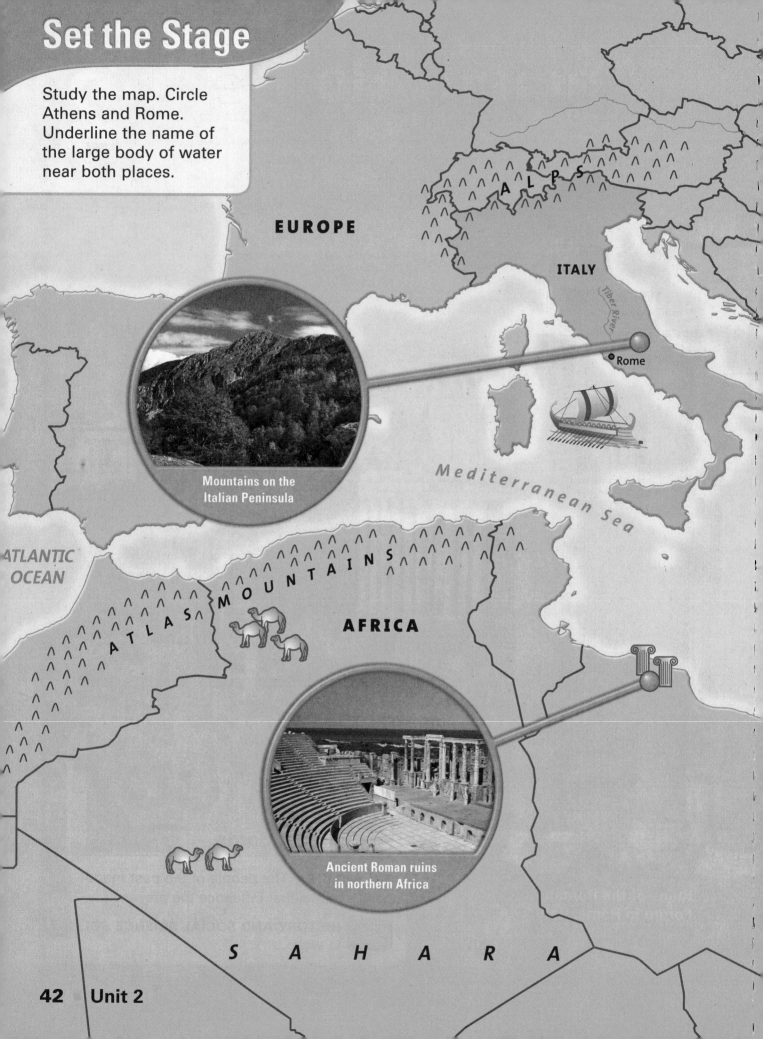

EUROPE

ALPS

ITALY

Tiber River

Rome

Mountains on the Italian Peninsula

Mediterranean Sea

ATLANTIC OCEAN

ATLAS MOUNTAINS

AFRICA

Ancient Roman ruins in northern Africa

SAHARA

The Lands Around Ancient Rome

EUROPE

Black Sea

Aegean Sea

GREECE

Athens

ASIA

The Parthenon of ancient Greece

Mediterranean Sea

The pyramids of ancient Egypt

Cairo

AFRICA

N
W   E
S

0   100   200 Miles
0   100   200 Kilometers

EGYPT

Nile River

Red Sea

Map Legend
- City
- ∧∧∧ Mountains
- —— Present-day border

Set the Stage

1 How is the Roman Colosseum on pages 44–45 different from the Greek Parthenon on page 27?

_____

_____

_____

2 Circle three kinds of art that Roman artists created.

A Family in Ancient Rome
Family life was very important to the ancient Romans.

Romans used arches to build the Colosseum, a famous building in Rome.

Roman Artists
Created mosaics, sculptures, and paintings

Cato the Elder
A leader who had new ideas about government

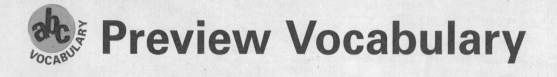

Preview Vocabulary

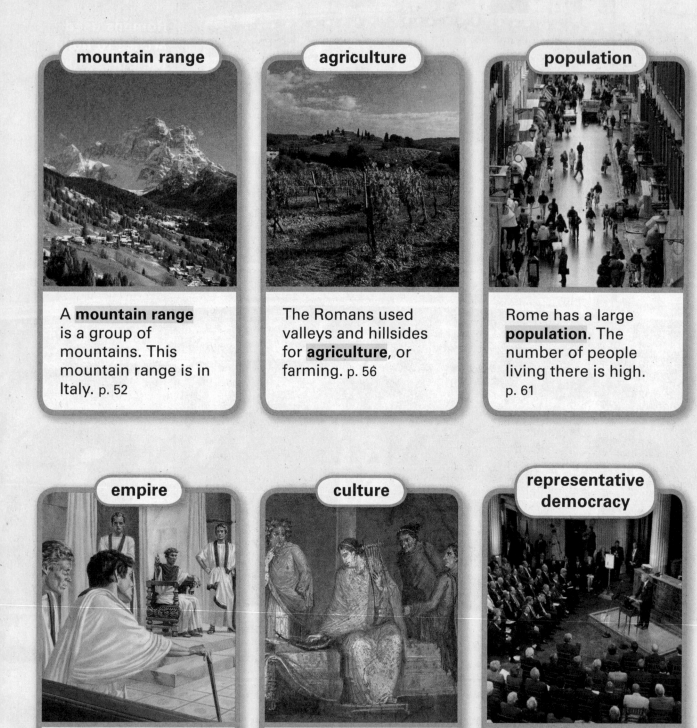

mountain range

A **mountain range** is a group of mountains. This mountain range is in Italy. p. 52

agriculture

The Romans used valleys and hillsides for **agriculture**, or farming. p. 56

population

Rome has a large **population**. The number of people living there is high. p. 61

empire

The Roman Empire was large. An **empire** is all the land and people ruled by a powerful nation. p. 62

culture

A **culture**, or way of life, is shared by members of a group. p. 64

representative democracy

In a **representative democracy**, people elect a smaller group to make the laws for everyone. p. 71

Reading Social Studies

⭐ Categorize and Classify
(Focus Skill)

Learn

Information is easier to use if facts are grouped into categories. A **category** is a group of things that are alike in some way. When you **classify** information, you sort it into categories. You place each thing into the group to which it belongs.

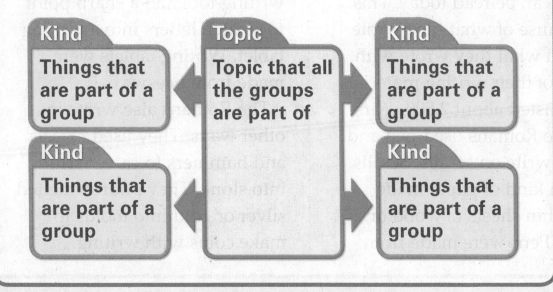

Kind	Topic	Kind
Things that are part of a group	**Topic that all the groups are part of**	**Things that are part of a group**

Kind	Kind
Things that are part of a group	**Things that are part of a group**

Practice

Read the paragraph. Circle each group of writers. Then underline the kinds of writing for each group. The first category has been done for you.

Different groups of Greeks wrote in ancient times. (Leaders) — Topic
wrote <u>letters</u>, <u>laws</u>, and <u>speeches</u>. Other writers created — Kind
stories, poems, and plays.

Read the following paragraphs. Then complete the activities below.

Roman Writing

Besides the Greeks, other ancient people recorded their history in writing. The ancient Romans did the same.

Much of what the Romans wrote can be read today. This is because of what they wrote on and what they wrote with. Some of their writing materials have lasted about 2,500 years.

Some Romans used pen and ink to write on scrolls. Scrolls were a kind of paper made from thin sheets of wood or reeds. Pens were made from reeds, bones, or bronze. Ink was made from a black powder mixed with water.

Other Romans used writing tools and writing tablets. A writing tool had a sharp point to scratch letters into a writing tablet. Writing tablets were made from beeswax.

The Romans also wrote in other ways. They used chisels and hammers to carve writing into stone. They poured melted silver or gold into molds to make coins with writing.

1. **Circle three categories of writing materials into which the information in the third paragraph can be classified.**

2. **Underline two categories of information described in the fourth paragraph.**

3. **What are two categories of writing into which the information in the fifth paragraph can be classified?**

_____

_____

_____

Rome's Location and Land

The ancient Greeks lived on a peninsula and on nearby islands in the Mediterranean Sea. The ancient Romans also lived on land near the Mediterranean Sea. Over time, the Romans united their villages to form the city of Rome. **Think about how the land of ancient Rome was like and different from the land of ancient Greece.**

Roman ruins in Italy, along the Mediterranean Sea

Essential Questions
✓ Where was ancient Rome located?
✓ What were the physical characteristics of ancient Rome?

 HISTORY AND SOCIAL SCIENCE SOL
3.4a, 3.4b

The Location of Ancient Rome

Long ago, a group of villages sat on seven hills above a beautiful river. In time, those villages joined and grew to become the city of Rome. Today, Rome is a city in the country of Italy.

Land and Sea

Italy is in southern Europe, not far to the west of Greece. Like Greece, most of Italy is a huge peninsula. Italy is made up of the Italian Peninsula and the islands of Sicily and Sardinia. The Italian Peninsula is shaped like a long, high-heeled boot. The "toe" of the boot almost touches Sicily.

The Italian Peninsula stretches into the Mediterranean Sea. About halfway up the peninsula is the Tiber (TY•ber) River. Ancient Rome was built along this river.

The Tiber River flows through the city of Rome.

❶ **What are two categories of information into which the location of ancient Rome can be classified?**

_____

_____

❷ **On what river was ancient Rome built? Why might people want to live by a river?**

_____

_____

❸ **Study the map on the next page. Circle the labels for the Italian Peninsula and the Mediterranean Sea. Then trace the Tiber River. Put an X on Rome.**

EUROPE

Map Legend
- • City
- ∧∧ Mountains
- — Present-day border

A L P S

Po River

ITALY

EUROPE

Corsica

A p e n n i n e s

Tiber River

Italian Peninsula

• Rome

Sardinia

Naples •

Cagliari •

N
W   E
S

0   50   100 Miles
0   50   100 Kilometers

Mediterranean   Sea

Sicily

AFRICA

Syracuse •

ASIA

EUROPE

AFRICA

Ancient Rome was located where Rome is today—on land near the Mediterranean Sea.

Rome's Physical Characteristics

The land that became Italy is similar in some ways to Greece. Like Greece, Italy is mostly a peninsula. It is surrounded by the Mediterranean Sea. However, Italy has features that make it different. It is a region with its own features. A **region** is a place that has common characteristics.

A Land of Mountains

Like Greece, Italy is a land of mountains. Italy has two large **mountain ranges**, or groups of mountains. The mountains in Italy are less rocky than those in Greece. This meant that early farmers in Italy could use more of the land. However, like Greece, Italy had limited amounts of rich soil. Still, the land was good for growing certain crops, such as olives and grapes.

In most of Italy, the climate is good for farming. Winter is usually not very cold. The region around Rome gets plenty of rain during winter. The other seasons are much drier in Italy. Summers can be very hot and dry.

The Land of Ancient Rome

Because of ancient Rome's location on the Italian Peninsula, the city was only about 15 miles from the Mediterranean Sea. Rome was built in a hilly area near mountains. The seven hills where the city began were next to the Tiber River.

Rome's best soil was found in its valleys. In ancient times, the seven hills were steep. Between the hills were small valleys. Flooding of the Tiber River left silt, or bits of rock and soil, in the valleys. This gave the valleys rich soil, just as the Nile River Valley of ancient Egypt had.

Mountains and hills cover much of the Italian Peninsula.

TextWork

7 What is the main idea of the first paragraph?

_____

_____

8 Underline the sentence that describes where Rome's best soil was located.

9 Use the words *hills* and *river* to write a description of ancient Rome's location.

_____

_____

_____

_____

_____

1. **SUMMARIZE** Where was ancient Rome located?

_____

_____

_____

_____

2. Use the word **region** in a sentence about Rome.

_____

_____

_____

_____

Circle the letter of the correct answer.

3. In which category do Sicily and Sardinia belong?

   A Hills

   B Islands

   C Peninsulas

   D Mountain ranges

4. Which physical characteristics BEST describe Rome's location?

   F On the Tiber River in Sicily

   G On a peninsula in Sardinia

   H On hills next to the Tiber River

   J On mountains next to the Tiber River

Draw a line connecting each feature on the left with the correct description on the right.

5. Italian Peninsula

6. ancient Rome

7. Tiber River

about halfway up the Italian Peninsula

stretches into the Mediterranean Sea

built about 15 miles from the sea

writing

✎ **Write a Paragraph** Write a paragraph that compares the physical features of Italy with those of Greece. Start with a good topic sentence.

ROME TOURIST MAP

Using Rome's Land

Lesson 2

The land where Rome began was a good place to settle. The Romans adapted their ways of life to the land and water. **Think about how land and water affected the ancient Romans.**

Terraces of olive trees in Italy

Essential Questions

✓ What were the physical characteristics of ancient Rome?

✓ How did the people of ancient Rome adapt to and change their environment to meet their needs?

 HISTORY AND SOCIAL SCIENCE SOL
3.4b, 3.4c

Ancient Romans and Their Environment

Like the Greeks, the ancient Romans adapted to their environment. They also changed it to better meet their needs.

Adapting to the Seven Hills

The Romans first settled on the seven hills for protection. The hills were steep. This protected the Romans from enemy attacks by land. The hills were also **inland**, or away from the coast. This protected the Romans from enemy attacks by sea.

Settling on the hills helped the Romans in other ways, too. It left more of the rich, flat land in the valleys for **agriculture**, or farming. Like the Greeks, the Romans built terraces on the sides of hills. They used them for raising crops and animals.

The ancient Romans adapted to their environment.

The Romans found useful natural resources among the hills as well. Several kinds of trees grew there. Stone was also plentiful. The Romans used these natural resources for building.

Adapting to the Tiber River

The Romans also adapted to the Tiber River. By settling on the hills, the Romans avoided the river's floodwaters. This kept them safe in times of flooding.

The Romans found important uses for the Tiber River, too. They used its water for farming, cooking, and drinking.

The Romans also used the Tiber River to reach the Mediterranean Sea for trading. They built a bridge over the river to connect trade routes over land. Ancient Rome became a center of trading by sea and by land.

4 Underline the sentence that explains how the Romans adapted to the flooding of the Tiber River.

5 How did the Romans use the Tiber River for trade on the Mediterranean Sea?

_____

_____

_____

6 Circle the names of the seven hills of ancient Rome shown on the map.

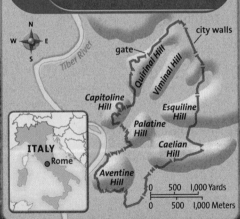

The Seven Hills of Ancient Rome

1. **SUMMARIZE** How did the ancient Romans adapt to the land and bodies of water near them?

_____

_____

_____

2. How did settling on the seven hills help the ancient Romans with **agriculture**?

_____

_____

_____

Circle the letter of the correct answer.

3. Which two natural resources were plentiful among the seven hills?

   A Stone and gold

   B Stone and salt

   C Trees and salt

   D Trees and stone

4. How did the Romans get to the Mediterranean Sea for trading?

   F They crossed a bridge.

   G They used the Tiber River.

   H They used only land routes.

   J They did not trade on the sea.

Draw a line connecting each category on the left with the correct information on the right.

5. trading   were found among the hills

6. agriculture   took place on the Mediterranean Sea

7. natural resources   was done in valleys and on terraces

activity

🖌 **Draw a Picture** Think of one way that the ancient Romans changed their environment. Then draw a picture of that change. Write a caption for your picture.

A farming tool from ancient Rome

Living and Working in Ancient Rome

Over time, ancient Rome grew in size and power. As the Romans' power spread, so did their way of life. People in faraway places began to follow Roman ways. **Think about how the ancient Romans lived and worked.**

A busy neighborhood in ancient Rome

Essential Questions

- ✓ What were the human characteristics of ancient Rome?
- ✓ How did the people of ancient Rome adapt to and change their environment to meet their needs?
- ✓ How do producers use natural, human, and capital resources in the production of goods and services?
- ✓ What are some of the goods and services produced in ancient Rome?
- ✓ What resources were used to produce goods and services in ancient Rome?

SOL HISTORY AND SOCIAL SCIENCE SOL
3.4b, 3.4c, 3.7

Early Roman farmers grew olives and other crops.

 TextWork

1 (Focus Skill) List three kinds of jobs in ancient Rome.

_____

_____

_____

2 What was ancient Rome's most important activity?

_____

3 Circle a product made from grains. Then underline two ways that Romans used olive oil.

Human Characteristics

Like the ancient Greeks, the Romans did different kinds of work. Many Romans were farmers, road builders, and traders.

Farmers

Farming was the most important activity in ancient Rome. Major crops included grains, olives, and grapes. The Romans used grains, such as wheat and barley, for making bread. They ate olives and grapes and used them for making other products. They cooked with olive oil and burned it in lamps for light.

Roman farmers also raised animals. Cows, sheep, and goats provided milk and cheese. Pigs provided most of the meat. Oxen and mules did work on farms.

Road Builders and Traders

Over time, the population of Rome grew. The **population** of a place is the number of people living there. The Romans had too little farmland to grow all the food they needed. To help meet this need, they began to trade with others.

To make trading easier, the Romans began to build roads. The Italian Peninsula is less mountainous than Greece. This allowed the Romans to build roads more easily than the Greeks could.

In time, Roman roads connected Rome to many parts of the peninsula. The Romans traded food products made from olives and grapes. They also traded the copper and iron they mined. In return, they got other foods and goods they needed.

The Romans became known for building roads. Some Roman roads still exist.

TextWork

❹ Underline the sentences that describe why the Romans began to trade. Then circle four products the Romans traded for other foods and goods.

❺ Why do you think Roman roads were able to last so long?

_____

_____

_____

A Roman coin

6 Underline the sentence that tells the main purpose of Roman roads.

7 Study the illustration. How was metal important to Roman armies?

_____

_____

_____

8 Study the map on page 63. Underline the names of the continents that the Roman Empire extended into.

Paved roads allowed Roman armies to travel quickly from place to place in the empire.

The Roman Empire

As Rome grew into a successful city, its power grew, too. Within about 200 years, Rome controlled the Italian Peninsula. In time, Rome became an empire. An **empire** is the land and people under the control of a powerful nation. The Roman Empire stretched around the Mediterranean Sea and beyond. It included the lands of ancient Egypt and Greece.

All Roads Lead to Rome

Besides using roads for trading, the Romans used them for moving their armies. In fact, this was the main purpose of the roads. Each time the Romans gained control of new land, they built roads on it. This helped them keep control of the land.

The Romans built thousands of miles of roads stretching out from Rome. The roads helped them increase trade. They also helped unite the people Rome ruled.

Shipbuilders

The Romans also traveled and traded on the Mediterranean Sea. They built ships to move armies and goods more quickly than they could by road. Transportation was an important service that helped Rome grow.

As sea travel grew, ships became more important. Producing ships required natural, human, and capital resources. Workers used tools to cut down trees to get the wood needed to build ships. They also used tools to cut wood for oars and sew cloth for sails. Ships moved by rowers using oars and by wind pushing the sails.

🔺 TextWork

❾ List three ways in which roads helped the Romans.

_____

_____

_____

❿ Is moving goods by ship a product or a service?

_____

⓫ Circle the three kinds of resources required for producing ships. Then draw a line from each circle to an example of the resource.

The Roman Empire

EUROPE

ASIA

Mediterranean Sea

AFRICA

Map Legend

◻ Roman lands ——— Present-day border

The Roman Forum was an open area surrounded by shops, temples, and other buildings.

TextWork

12 (Focus Skill) List four categories of jobs for early Roman workers.

_____

_____

_____

_____

13 Underline the sentence that explains what allowed Roman workers to produce new goods and services.

Life in Ancient Rome

The Roman Empire included people from different cultures. A **culture** is a way of life shared by members of a group. The Romans exchanged ideas and goods with these cultures. Many parts of Roman culture came from the Greeks.

City Life

Rome was the center of Roman culture, trade, and government. The city was filled with markets, temples, theaters, and sports arenas. The Romans used ideas from Greek architecture in many buildings.

Most workers in early Rome farmed, fished, built ships, or made pottery. In time, traders brought goods and resources from other places. Workers then used these for producing new goods and services.

They used metals from Spain and Britain to make weapons. Roman armies used these weapons in wars.

Home Life

Most Romans lived in apartments without kitchens or running water. They carried water from public fountains. They bought meals from shops or cooked outside on small grills. People ate mostly bread, fruit, vegetables, and cheese.

Wealthy Romans lived in large homes with running water and gardens. They ate foods from all over the empire. Workers did all the cooking and cleaning for them.

Roman children began their education at home. When a boy was old enough, he learned to do his father's job. A girl learned about running a home from her mother. Only boys from wealthy families attended school.

TextWork

14 How did Roman trade help the Roman armies?

_____

_____

15 Scan this page. Circle one way life in ancient Rome was different from your life today.

A writing tool and tablet

Children in History

Roman Children at Play

Roman children liked to play. They enjoyed playing with toys. Popular toys included balls, dolls, marbles, stilts, and kites. Children also liked to build models. Board games were popular, too, especially tic-tac-toe. Dogs and birds were the most common pets.

Make It Relevant **What games do you play that Roman children also played?**

1. **SUMMARIZE** What were the main human characteristics of ancient Rome?

   _____

   _____

   _____

2. Write a sentence about the earlier civilization that affected Rome's **culture** the most.

   _____

   _____

   _____

Circle the letter of the correct answer.

3. What were the major crops of ancient Rome?

   A Peppers, olives, and grapes

   B Grains, squash, and grapes

   C Grains, olives, and grapes

   D Rice, olives, and grapes

4. In ancient Rome, providing transportation was an important—

   F natural resource

   G good

   H capital resource

   J service

Draw a line connecting each kind of resource on the left with the correct shipbuilding resource on the right.

5. natural resource   tools

6. human resource   wood

7. capital resource   workers

activity

Make a Chart Review this lesson. List five goods and five services produced in ancient Rome. Organize your list into a chart. Divide the chart into two parts—*goods* and *services*.

Contributions of Ancient Rome

Like the Greeks, the ancient Romans also made important contributions to architecture and government. Their contributions in these and other areas affect people today. **Think about the contributions the ancient Romans made.**

Roman ruins in southern France

Essential Questions

✓ What styles in architecture used today came from ancient Rome?

✓ What principles of government from ancient Rome are part of our government?

HISTORY AND SOCIAL SCIENCE SOL
3.1

Architecture and Arts

The ancient Romans are famous for their architecture and art. They took many ideas from other cultures. Then they found ways to improve them.

Columns and Arches

Like the Greeks, Roman architects used columns in their buildings. The Romans, however, were the first to use arches widely in buildings, domes, bridges, and aqueducts (A•kwuh•duhkts). **Aqueducts** are human-made pipelines or channels used to carry water to cities.

The Romans also made earlier kinds of concrete stronger. This allowed them to make larger and longer-lasting buildings. Parts of Roman buildings still stand today!

TextWork

1 (Focus Skill) Underline four ways the Romans used arches.

2 How might aqueducts have been important to life in ancient Rome?

_____

_____

_____

Rome's largest arena was the Colosseum (kah•luh•SEE•uhm). It could hold 50,000 people. The Colosseum was used for entertainment, such as races and circuses.

The Arts

Like the Greeks, the Romans displayed art on their buildings. Roman mosaics decorated everything from homes to temples. The Romans were probably the first people to use mosaics on floors.

Roman sculptures looked like those of the Greeks. In fact, Greek artists living in Rome made many sculptures there. Sculptures of Roman leaders could be found throughout the Roman Empire.

Roman paintings showed scenes of animals, landscapes, daily life, and war. This art tells us much about Roman lives.

A Roman mosaic of a dog

TextWork

❸ Circle the name of Rome's largest arena.

❹ (Focus Skill) List three categories of Roman art.

_____

_____

_____

❺ Why do you think the Roman Empire had so many sculptures of its leaders?

_____

_____

Roman architects used many arches to build the Colosseum.

In the Roman Republic, citizens elected leaders to represent them.

 **TextWork**

6 What new kind of government did the Romans create?

_____

7 How is a representative democracy different from the direct democracy in ancient Greece?

_____

_____

_____

Roman Government

The Romans contributed new ideas about government. About 2,500 years ago, powerful kings ruled Roman lands. These kings were not Romans. One king treated the Romans very badly. To stop this, the Romans forced the king and his family out of Rome. The Romans then decided to form a government in which no one person could gain total power.

The Roman Republic

The Romans formed a new kind of government called a republic. In a **republic**, citizens elect leaders to represent them.

The Roman Republic was a representative democracy. A **representative democracy** is a government in which people vote for, or elect, a smaller group of citizens to make the rules and laws for everyone.

The Three Parts of Government

Two consuls (KAHN•suhlz) led the Roman government, taking the place of the king. They shared power so that no one consul could have too much power. They led the Republic and its army. They also acted as judges and suggested laws.

The second part of the government was the senate. It was the most powerful part. These 300 free men advised the consuls. All citizens could serve in the senate.

The third part of government was the assemblies. The assemblies elected the consuls and helped make the laws. As with the senate, all citizens could serve.

TextWork

8 List the three main parts of the Roman Republic.

_____

_____

_____

9 Why did the Romans have two consuls instead of one?

_____

_____

Biography

Citizenship

Cato the Elder

Cato the Elder was a soldier and leader of the Roman Republic. He worked hard at making the Republic strong. As a soldier, he helped defeat Rome's enemies. As a leader, he served the Republic, including as consul. Cato encouraged Romans to be honest and to live simple lives.

⑩ Circle three ideas from Roman architecture that are still used today.

⑪ Underline the part of the United States Congress for which the Roman senate was the model.

⑫ Study the chart on page 73. How was Rome's contribution to government different from Greece's?

_____

_____

The United States Congress

Contributions Today

The ancient Greeks and Romans made important contributions to many areas of life. Some of their contributions were alike, while others were different. It is important to understand how the ideas of the ancient Greeks and Romans affect our lives today.

Roman-style architecture can be found around the world today. Many buildings in the United States, including Virginia, use Roman architecture. Roman ideas for arches, domes, and concrete are still used.

Like the Roman Republic, the United States is a republic and a representative democracy. The Roman assembly was the model for the United States House of Representatives. The Roman senate was the model for the United States Senate. The Senate and the House are both part of the United States Congress.

The United States Capitol has Roman-style architecture.

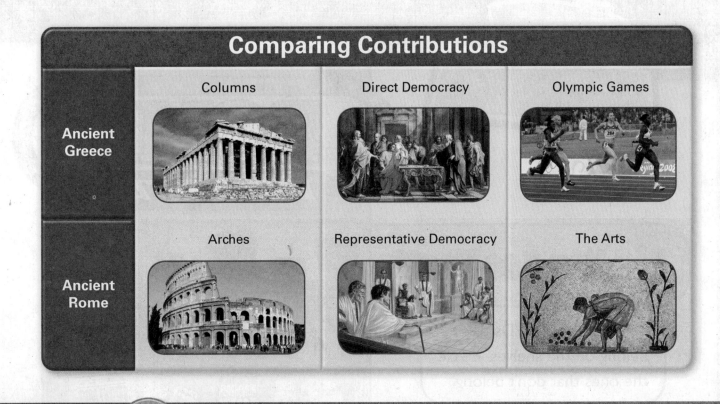

Comparing Contributions

	Columns	Direct Democracy	Olympic Games
Ancient Greece			
	Arches	Representative Democracy	The Arts
Ancient Rome			

Lesson 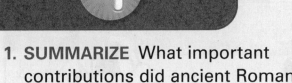 Review

1. **SUMMARIZE** What important contributions did ancient Romans make that affect us today?

_____

_____

2. Use the word **republic** in a sentence about ancient Rome and the United States.

_____

_____

Circle the letter of the correct answer.

3. Which did the ancient Romans use to carry water to cities?

   A Arch

   B Column

   C Aqueduct

   D Dome

A Roman sculpture

writing

✎ **Give a Speech** Choose a contribution from ancient Rome. Then write a speech about how it affects your life. Give your speech to your class.

Fun With Social Studies

ROME DVD RENTAL

Did You See That?

Some of these DVDs don't belong on the shelves. Circle the ones that don't belong.

SEVEN HILLS CHIHUAHUA

ON THE BANKS OF THE NILE

Bridge Over the Tiber River

Sleepless in Athens

20,000 Leagues Under the Mediterranean Sea

THE HUNCHBACK OF CRETE

The Muppets take the Italian Peninsula

SEE A GREAT MOVIE ABOUT ANCIENT ROME TONIGHT

Fill It In

What's the word? Add the missing letters.

VOCABULARY

Word	Clue
r □ gi □ n	an area that is different from other areas
□ gr □ c □□ tu □ e	farming
p □ pul □□ io □	the number of people living in a place
c □ lt □ r □	a way of life shared by members of a group
□ qu □ du □ t	a human-made pipeline or channel used to carry water to a city

74 ▪ Unit 2

Roaming Around

Calvin collects buttons. Draw a line connecting each button to the picture it describes.

All roads lead to Rome

See the races! 50,000 tickets available!

Making art, piece by piece

Bringing water to your city

Review and Test Prep

The Big Idea

The people of the past made contributions that influence the present.

Summarize the Unit

Categorize and Classify Complete the graphic organizer to show that you can categorize and classify information about ancient Rome.

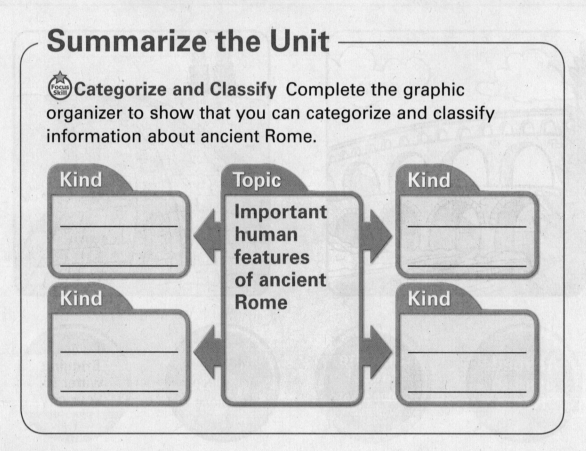

Kind _____

Topic: Important human features of ancient Rome

Kind _____

Kind _____

Kind _____

Use Vocabulary

Complete each sentence with a vocabulary term from the Word Bank.

1. The Roman Republic was also a _____.

2. _____ was the most important activity in ancient Rome.

3. The Italian Peninsula has two large _____.

4. Many ideas of ancient Roman _____ came from the ancient Greeks.

Word Bank

mountain ranges p. 52

agriculture p. 56

population p. 61

culture p. 64

representative democracy p. 71

Think About It

Circle the letter of the correct answer.

5.

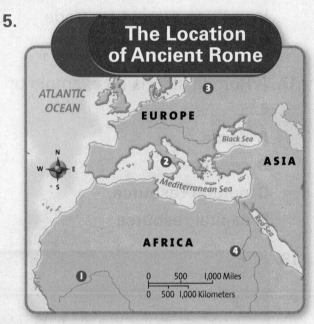

The Location of Ancient Rome

Which number shows where the city of ancient Rome was located?

A 1

B 2

C 3

D 4

6. Which large body of water was near ancient Rome?

F Atlantic Ocean

G Baltic Sea

H Mediterranean Sea

J Rhine River

7. Along which river was ancient Rome built?

A Nile River

B Tiber River

C Yellow River

D Rhine River

8.
- a river
- many hills
- limited rich soil

These are examples of—

F human resources

G capital resources

H human characteristics

J physical characteristics

9. Ancient Rome was built on—

A five hills

B six hills

C seven hills

D eight hills

10. Where was MOST of the rich soil in ancient Rome located?

F Along the sea

G In the valleys

H On hillsides

J On mountains

11. The ancient Romans adapted hillsides to farming by—

A settling in the valleys

B flooding the hills

C spreading silt

D building terraces

12. Which natural resource was plentiful in ancient Rome?

F Stone

G Rich soil

H Gold

J Diamonds

13.

> The ancient Romans used the Mediterranean Sea for trading.

In this sentence, trading is an example of a—

A good

B service

C natural resource

D capital resource

14. Farmers, road builders, and other workers are examples of—

F natural resources

G human resources

H goods

J services

15. In ancient Rome, which was a product of olives?

A Oil for cooking

B Bread

C Feed for animals

D Juice

16. The MAIN purpose of early Roman roads was to—

F provide a route to the sea

G move travelers

H provide a route for trade

J move armies

17. A Roman ship is an example of a—

A dome

B service

C natural resource

D capital resource

18.

Which feature shown in the photograph was the first to be widely used by the Romans?

F Columns

G Arches

H Terraces

J Domes

19. Aqueducts were used to—

A carry water to cities

B move small boats

C carry silt to valleys

D hold back floodwaters

20.

> - mosaic
> - sculpture
> - painting

These are examples of—

F architecture

G columns

H artwork

J buildings

21. Before the Roman Republic, who ruled Roman lands?

A A king

B A consul

C A senate

D An assembly

22. The Roman Republic was a—

F government of four parts

G direct democracy

H group of kings

J representative democracy

Answer these questions.

23. What goods and services were important in ancient Rome?

_____

_____

_____

24. What are three characteristics of Roman architecture that are still used in buildings today?

_____

_____

_____

25. What ideas of government from ancient Romans are part of our government today?

_____

_____

_____

Running an ancient Roman trading business is no easy task! You and Eco will learn how hard it is as you help a Roman trader buy and sell goods. Can you succeed at these challenges? Go online to play the game now.

HMH

ECO

Show What You Know

✎ Writing Write a Summary
Write a summary describing the contributions of the ancient Romans that affect people today. Use information from this unit and from other resource materials in your summary.

🖌 Activity A Wall of Murals
On a large sheet of paper, draw a picture showing life in ancient Rome. In your scene, include examples of both physical and human characteristics of Rome. Also show at least one contribution that still affects people today. Add labels or captions to your picture. Display your picture on a wall of murals.

The Empire of Mali

A mosque in
Jenné, Mali

Spotlight on Standards

THE BIG IDEA The location of a place can affect its history.

SOL **HISTORY AND SOCIAL SCIENCE SOL**
3.2, 3.4a, 3.4b, 3.4c, 3.7

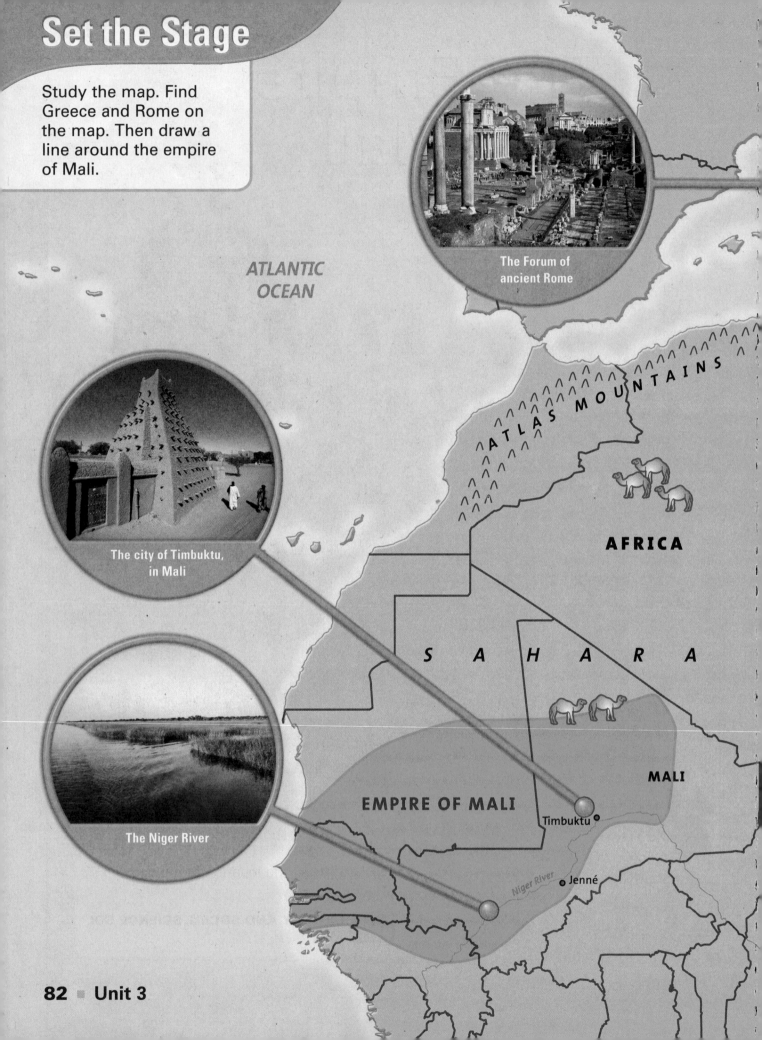

Set the Stage

Study the map. Find Greece and Rome on the map. Then draw a line around the empire of Mali.

The Forum of ancient Rome

ATLANTIC OCEAN

ATLAS MOUNTAINS

AFRICA

The city of Timbuktu, in Mali

S A H A R A

MALI

The Niger River

EMPIRE OF MALI

Timbuktu

Niger River

Jenné

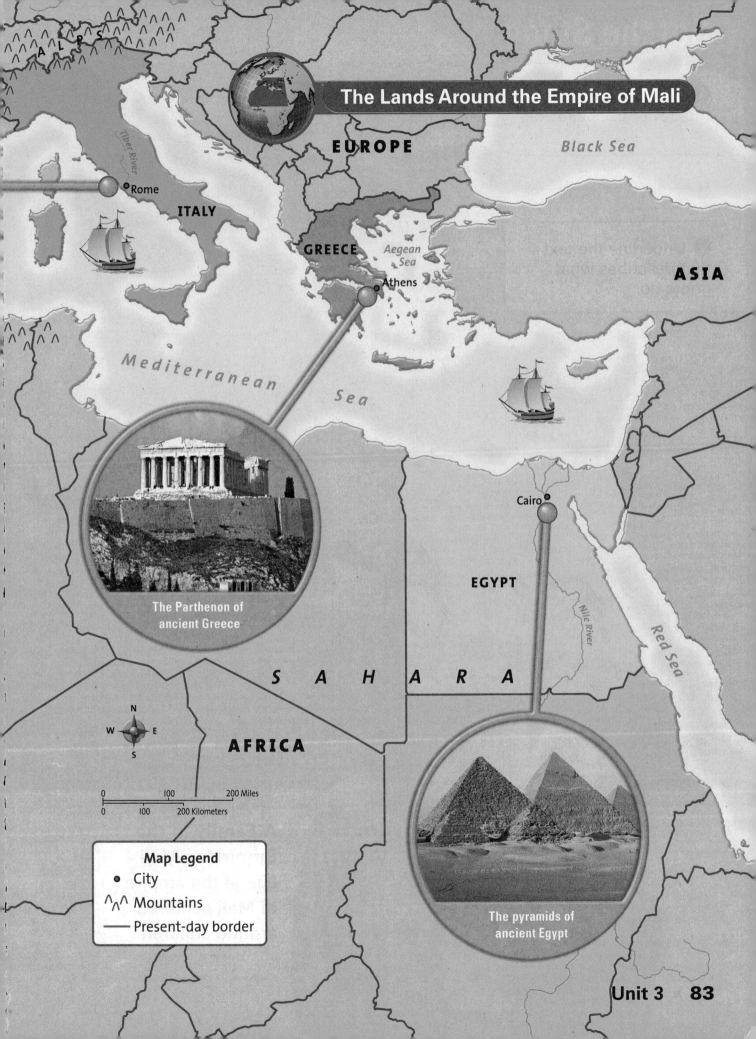

The Lands Around the Empire of Mali

EUROPE

Black Sea

Tiber River

Rome

ITALY

GREECE

Athens

Aegean
Sea

ASIA

Mediterranean

Sea

The Parthenon of
ancient Greece

Cairo

EGYPT

Nile River

Red Sea

S A H A R A

N
W   E
S

AFRICA

0   100   200 Miles
0   100   200 Kilometers

The pyramids of
ancient Egypt

Map Legend
- City
- ∧∧∧ Mountains
- —— Present-day border

A L P S

Set the Stage

1 Why do you think the trader uses camels?

_____

_____

_____

2 Underline the text that describes what griots do.

A Family in the Empire of Mali
Life in the empire of Mali centered around children.

84

A trader and his camels cross the Sahara in Africa.

Griots
Storytellers in West Africa who pass on history and ways of life

Sundiata
An important leader of the empire of Mali

abc Preview Vocabulary

desert

The Sahara is a **desert** in Africa. It has a very dry climate. p. 90

savanna
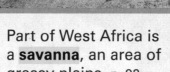

Part of West Africa is a **savanna**, an area of grassy plains. p. 92

barter

West Africans were able to **barter** gold for salt. They traded these goods without using money. p. 101

generation

A **generation** is the time between the birth of parents and the birth of their children. p. 102

tradition

Telling stories was a tradition in West Africa. A **tradition** is a custom passed on to others. p. 103

crossroads

A **crossroads** is a place with a central location. p. 108

Reading Social Studies

⭐ Focus Skill Cause and Effect

Learn

A **cause** is something that makes something else happen. An **effect** is something that happens as a result of a cause. Words and phrases such as *because*, *as a result*, *since*, and *so* can help you identify why something happens. Sometimes a cause can have more than one effect.

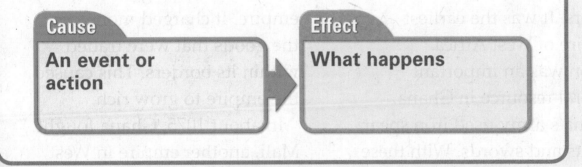

Cause		Effect
An event or action	→	What happens

Practice

Read the paragraphs. Circle the cause and underline the effect or effects in each paragraph. The first paragraph has been done for you.

After many years, different groups within Rome fought each other for power. As a result, Rome started to weaken. **Cause** **Effect**

Outside groups began to attack Rome. Because of this, Rome needed a larger army. Rome collected more money from its people to pay for the army.

Apply

Read the following paragraphs. Then complete the activities below.

The Empire of Ghana

As Rome weakened, a strong empire grew in Africa. Ghana gained power around the year 700. Ghana was located between the Niger (NY•jer) and Senegal (seh•nih•GAWL) Rivers. It was the earliest empire of West Africa.

Iron was an important natural resource in Ghana. Ghana's army used iron spear points and swords. With these weapons, Ghana was able to protect itself. Its neighbors used weapons made of wood and stone.

Farmers also used tools made of iron. Because of these tools, farmers grew more crops.

Ghana was located between salt and gold mines. As a result, it became a strong trading empire. It charged money on the goods that were traded within its borders. This caused the empire to grow rich.

In about 1075, Ghana fought Mali, another empire in West Africa. Ghana lost and became weak. As a result, the empire of Mali took over the empire of Ghana 150 years later.

1. **Underline the effect of farmers using tools made of iron.**

2. **What caused Ghana to become a strong and rich trading empire?**

_____

_____

_____

3. **Circle the reason Mali was later able to rule Ghana.**

Mali's Location and Land

Between 700 and 1400, the empire of Mali spread over much of the western part of Africa. West Africa includes regions with different physical characteristics. **Think about what you might learn about the location and land of the empire of Mali.**

Much of Mali's land is dry.

Essential Questions
✓ Where was the empire of Mali located?
✓ What were the physical characteristics of West Africa?

 HISTORY AND SOCIAL SCIENCE SOL
3.4a, 3.4b

❶ Scan the text on pages 90–91. Underline the region of Africa where the empire of Mali was located.

❷ What kinds of land are found in Africa?

_____

_____

_____

_____

The Location of the Empire of Mali

At different times in the past, West Africa was ruled by great empires. One of the richest was Mali. It reached its largest size about 800 years ago. Today, the country of Mali is located on land that was once part of the empire of Mali.

A Western Region of Africa

Africa is the second-largest continent. It is south of Europe and the Mediterranean Sea. Africa has deserts, grasslands, forests, and mountains. The Sahara, the world's largest desert, is in Africa. A **desert** is a place where the climate is dry. South of the Sahara are grasslands and forests.

African Grassland

The Sahara

African Forest

The empire of Mali was located in West Africa, the western region of Africa. The Sahara bordered the northern part of the empire. The Atlantic Ocean formed its western border. The Niger and Gambia Rivers ran near the region's southern border.

 **TextWork**

❸ On the globe, draw a box around the continent Mali is found on. On the map, trace a line around the empire of Mali.

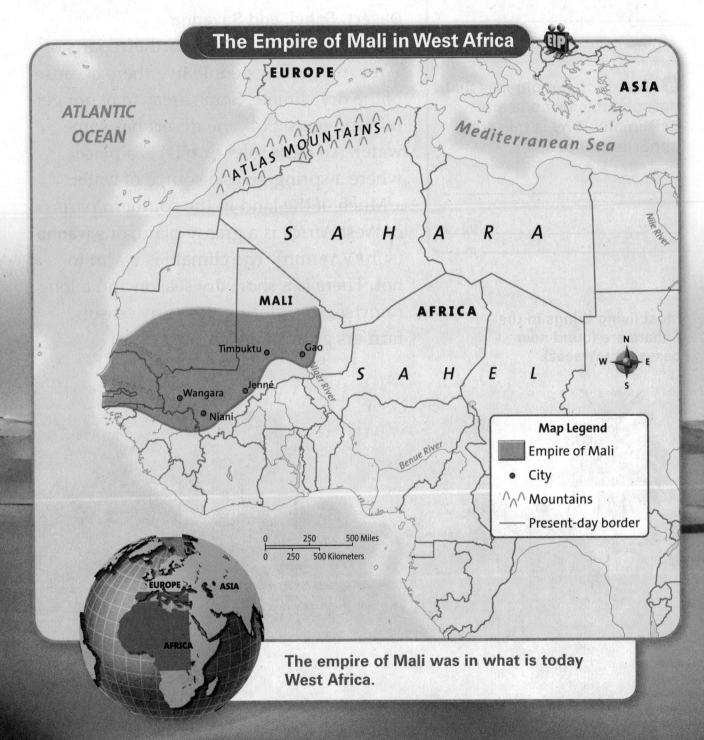

The empire of Mali was in what is today West Africa.

④ Study the photograph. How is the oasis different from the rest of the Sahara?

_____

_____

⑤ Underline the phrases that describe the savanna and its climate. Why is this area important to people?

_____

_____

Most living things in the Sahara are found near oases (oh•AY•seez).

West Africa's Physical Characteristics

Because West Africa is so large, it has different kinds of physical characteristics. The landforms and climates are very different in different parts of West Africa.

Desert, Sahel, and Savanna

The Sahara covers the northern parts of West Africa. Few people live there because of the dry climate. Some areas may not get rain for years. Still, the desert has some water. An **oasis** (oh•AY•sis) is a place where a spring gives a source of water.

Much of the land in the southern parts of West Africa is a grassy plain, or **savanna** (suh•VA•nuh). The climate is warm to hot. There is a short dry season and a long rainy season. During the rainy season, farmers grow many crops.

The Physical Characteristics of West Africa

Sahara	Sahel	Savanna

Three different kinds of land are found in West Africa.

Between the savanna and desert areas of West Africa is the Sahel (SA•hil). Like the Sahara, the Sahel is mainly sand. However, this land has short grasses and small plants. Most of it is too dry for farming, though. Only in the southern Sahel can some crops grow.

The Niger and Senegal Rivers

Two important rivers in West Africa are the Niger and the Senegal. The Niger flows across the region for more than 2,500 miles. The Senegal is about 1,000 miles long.

Because of flooding, the land near both rivers is fertile, or good for growing crops. During the time of the empire of Mali, the rivers were like highways. People used them to travel and to move goods.

The land of West Africa also has natural resources. For example, gold was found near the Niger River Valley.

TextWork

6 Circle the text that tells how the Sahara and the Sahel are alike.

7 (Focus Skill) What effect does flooding have on the land near the Niger and Senegal Rivers?

_____

_____

8 Underline the text that tells how people of the empire of Mali used the Niger and Senegal Rivers.

1. **SUMMARIZE** Where was the empire of Mali located?

_____

_____

_____

2. Use the word **desert** in a sentence about the location of the empire of Mali.

_____

_____

_____

3. How were the Niger and Senegal Rivers used in the empire of Mali?

_____

_____

_____

Circle the letter of the correct answer.

4. Which kind of land in West Africa is best for growing crops?

   A Sahel

   B savanna

   C Sahara

   D mountains

Draw a line connecting each physical characteristic of West Africa on the left with the correct description on the right.

5. Sahara

6. savanna

7. Sahel

between the savanna and the desert

dry area that receives little or no rain

grassy plain

activity

Make a Mural Make a mural that shows the physical characteristics of West Africa. On a posterboard, draw pictures of West Africa's land, bodies of water, and climate.

Meerkats in West Africa

Using Mali's Land

West Africa's land is different in different places. The people of Mali learned how to use each kind of land. **Think about how West Africa's land affected the people of Mali.**

People in Mali use the land to grow onions.

Essential Questions
- ✓ What were the physical characteristics of West Africa?
- ✓ How did the people of Mali adapt to and change their environment to meet their needs?

HISTORY AND SOCIAL SCIENCE SOL
3.4b, 3.4c

Today, farmers still change the environment to irrigate crops.

Living in West Africa

People in the empire of Mali adapted their way of life to their environment. They learned to live in a hot, mostly dry region. They changed the land to meet their needs.

Making the Most of the Land

In the savanna, the Niger River flooded during the rainy season. The floods left behind fertile soil on the land along the river. The people of Mali used this rich soil to grow grains, such as rice and millet.

To farm, people cleared away grasses. They also dug ditches to store floodwater. During the dry season, they were then able to **irrigate**, or bring water to, their fields. This was similar to the way the ancient Egyptians farmed along the Nile River.

In contrast, the Sahel had little water. Its soil was mostly dry and sandy. There were few places where people could farm. The people of Mali used this land to raise livestock, such as cattle, goats, and sheep.

Making the Most of Natural Resources

Both gold and salt were important natural resources in the empire of Mali. People dug mines to get gold and salt, as well as iron and copper.

People dug gold mines near a city called Wangara, far to the south. Often, they traded gold for other resources.

For the people of Mali, salt was worth as much as gold. They needed salt to stay healthy. They also used it to **preserve** food, or to keep it from spoiling. People mined salt from beneath the Sahara. Because salt was so important, it was traded for gold.

TextWork

4 (Focus Skill) What caused the people living in the Sahel to have few places to farm?

_____

_____

5 Study the photographs on pages 96–97. Circle the person irrigating crops. Put a box around the person gathering salt.

6 Underline the sentence that tells how the people of Mali changed the environment to get salt and gold.

Salt is still an important natural resource in the Sahara.

1. **SUMMARIZE** How did the people of Mali make the most of West Africa's physical characteristics?

_____

_____

_____

2. Use the word **irrigate** to describe one way people in the empire of Mali changed their land.

_____

_____

_____

3. What natural resources were important to the people of the empire of Mali?

_____

_____

_____

Circle the letter of the correct answer.

4. Which is a way the people of Mali changed their environment?

   A They wore loose clothing.

   B They dug mines.

   C They traveled on rivers.

   D They used camels.

Draw a line connecting each activity on the left with the correct description of the part of West Africa where that activity was mostly done.

5. Raising livestock   fertile land of the savanna

6. Mining natural resources   dry land of the Sahel

7. Growing grains   under the ground

activity

📝 **Draw a Picture** List ways in which people in the empire of Mali changed their environment. Then make a picture of one of those changes.

The people of Mali wore gold jewelry.

Life in the Empire of Mali

People today trade in this market in Jenné (jeh•NAY) like they did long ago.

People in the empire of Mali worked at many jobs. There were farmers, miners, and traders. There were also storytellers and rulers. **Think about what life was like in the empire of Mali.**

Essential Questions

✓ What were the human characteristics of West Africa?

✓ Why were storytellers so important in the empire of Mali?

✓ What do we know about the leaders of the empire of Mali?

✓ What are some of the goods and services produced in the West African empire of Mali?

✓ What resources (natural, human, capital) were used to produce goods and services in the West African empire of Mali?

SOL **HISTORY AND SOCIAL SCIENCE SOL**
3.2, 3.4b, 3.7

Human Characteristics

Like Greece and Rome, Mali had different human characteristics. There were villages, cities, mines, and trade routes. There were different kinds of jobs, too. Most people in Mali were farmers, miners, or traders. They all used different kinds of resources to produce goods and services. They all changed the land.

Farmers

Most farmers lived on the savanna. To prepare the land, farmers burned off the savanna's grasses. Then, in May and June, they planted grains, such as rice and millet. They also planted beans and peanuts. In November and December, farmers harvested the crops. They grew enough food for their needs and for trade goods.

TextWork

❶ Underline the crops that farmers planted on the savanna.

❷ What did farmers do in November and December?

_____

_____

❸ Study the illustration. Draw a circle around a person making a good. Then describe how a person in the scene is providing a service.

_____

_____

The people of Mali traded goods and services in markets.

Miners

Mali had many natural resources, such as salt, gold, and iron. People traded these resources. They also used them to make goods. For example, they made tools from iron and made jewelry from gold.

Miners dug and worked in the mines to get natural resources. The miners were human resources. They used tools, or capital resources, to do their work.

Traders

The rulers of the empire of Mali controlled all the trade in West Africa. Traders bartered for gold, salt, and other products. To **barter** is to trade goods or services for other goods or services without using money. Cities throughout the empire became centers of trade. The traders provided a service that helped people get the goods they needed.

TextWork

4 Underline the text that tells what natural resources were found in Mali. What kind of resources were the workers? the tools they used?

_____

_____

5 Give an example of items people in the empire of Mali may have used to barter.

_____

_____

Griots used storytelling to pass on Mali's customs and history.

TextWork

6 Underline the text that tells how we know the histories of West African empires.

7 Circle the word *griot* and its definition. In what ways may griots share their culture's history?

_____

_____

_____

_____

Oral Traditions

The West African empires had no written languages. Most of what we know about their histories comes from stories they passed on from one generation to the next. A **generation** is the time between the birth of parents and the birth of their children.

Griots

A **griot** (GREE•oh) is a West African storyteller who passes on his or her culture's history. *Griot* comes from a French word that means "keeper of memories." Griots tell stories, sing songs, recite poetry, and dance.

Mamadou Kouyate, a griot today, says, "I derive [get] my knowledge from my father . . . who also got it from his father."

The Role of Griots in the Empire of Mali

Griots were important in the empire of Mali. They knew about Mali's history and traditions. A **tradition** is a custom that is passed on to others. Storytelling is an oral, or spoken, tradition.

Rulers often turned to griots for advice. Griots used their knowledge of the past to help rulers solve problems. Because of their wisdom, griots held high positions.

Griots had other roles as well. Some served as the empire's musicians. They sang and played a drum called a *djembe* or a stringed instrument called a *kora*. Others had the job of teaching princes. They made sure the princes knew Mali's history and traditions. Griots also started new celebrations. They held one each year for planting and another for harvesting.

 **TextWork**

8 Why were griots important to Mali's history and traditions?

_____

_____

9 (Focus Skill) Underline the text that tells what caused griots to hold high positions in the empire of Mali.

10 Circle other roles that griots had in the empire of Mali.

A griot

A djembe

A kora

EIP

Governing the Empire of Mali

Mali was ruled by rich and powerful men. They were kings called *mansas*. The mansas brought riches to the empire by controlling trade. In time, Mali became one of the largest and richest empires in West Africa. It was an important center of trade.

Sundiata

Sundiata (sun•JAHT•ah) was the first *mansa*. He **conquered**, or took over, many lands. This caused the empire to grow. Wisely, Sundiata let kings who lost to him keep ruling their own lands. However, they had to promise to obey Sundiata and pay taxes. A tax is money people pay to the government. This helped the empire of Mali become very rich.

TextWork

⓫ Circle the word that means almost the same as *king*.

⓬ Underline the text that tells how Sundiata treated the rulers of lands he conquered.

⓭ (Focus Skill) What caused the empire of Mali to become rich?

_____

_____

Biography

Fairness

Sundiata

Sundiata's people were conquered by a neighboring king. Sundiata raised an army and freed them. After this, he became mansa. Sundiata was a wise ruler. He treated his people fairly. The laws were the same for everyone. During Sundiata's rule, the empire became rich and powerful.

Time

1210 Born — **1255** Died

1230 Sundiata becomes king of Mali

This map of the empire of Mali from 1375 includes a portrait of Mansa Musa.

Mansa Musa

After Sundiata died, several weak leaders ruled Mali. Then Mansa Musa came to power in 1307. During his rule, the trade cities of Gao (GOW) and Timbuktu (tim•buhk•TOO) became part of Mali.

In 1324, Mansa Musa went on a pilgrimage, or religious trip. Mansa Musa was a Muslim. Muslims follow the religion of Islam. On his trip, Mansa Musa traveled to the Muslim city of Mecca in Southwest Asia. Along the way, he gave gold to the poor. People were amazed at his kindness and how much gold he had.

Mansa Musa saw how important learning was to the people of Southwest Asia. Upon his return, he turned Timbuktu into a center of learning. It also became a center for Muslim culture. People came from near and far to teach and to learn.

 **TextWork**

⑭ List two trade cities that became part of the empire of Mali.

_____

_____

⑮ Underline the reason people thought Mansa Musa was kind.

⑯ Look at the map. Circle clues from the drawing of Mansa Musa that show that he was rich and powerful.

1. **SUMMARIZE** What was life like in the empire of Mali?

_____

_____

_____

2. How are **barter** and trade related?

_____

_____

3. Why were griots important to the empire of Mali?

_____

_____

_____

4. What were three natural resources that were important to Mali?

_____

_____

_____

Draw a line connecting each word on the left with the correct definition on the right.

5. griot

6. generation

7. tradition

a custom passed on to others

a storyteller who passes on his or her culture

the time between the birth of parents and the birth of their children

writing

✎ **Write a Story** Use resources, such as books or the Internet, to collect and record information about one of Mali's rulers. Write a story about the ruler. Present it to the class as if you were a griot.

This sculpture shows a soldier from the empire of Mali.

Centers of Trade and Learning

The people of the empire of Mali made good use of their land's resources. They also used the empire's location to build up trade. As a result, the empire became wealthy, or very rich. Its cities became important centers of trade and learning. **Think about why places in the empire of Mali became centers of trade and learning.**

Timbuktu was a center of trade and learning during the time of the empire of Mali.

Essential Questions

✓ Why was the empire of Mali so wealthy?

✓ What are some of the goods and services produced in the West African empire of Mali?

✓ What resources (natural, human, capital) were used to produce goods and services in the West African empire of Mali?

SOL **HISTORY AND SOCIAL SCIENCE SOL**
3.2, 3.7

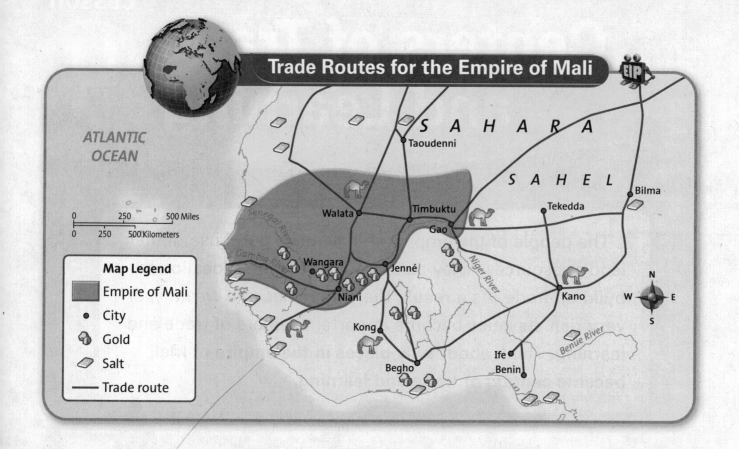

ATLANTIC OCEAN

Map Legend

- ▨ Empire of Mali
- • City
- 🪙 Gold
- ⬦ Salt
- — Trade route

SAHARA

Taoudenni

SAHEL

Bilma

Walata

Timbuktu

Tekedda

Gao

Senegal River

Gambia River

Wangara

Jenné

Niger River

Kano

Niani

Kong

Ife

Benin

Begho

Benue River

N W E S

TextWork

❶ On the map, circle the cities that were on trade routes in the empire of Mali.

❷ (Focus Skill) Scan the first paragraph. What caused Mali to become an important center of trade?

_____

_____

A Crossroads of Trade

Mali's resources and location made it an important center of trade. Mali lay between the sources of salt in the Sahara and the gold mines of West Africa. In Mali, traders exchanged these natural resources. They then took them to sell in other places. In this way, Mali became a crossroads of trade. A **crossroads** is a place with a central location. Mali became one of the largest and wealthiest empires in West Africa.

The mansas taxed all goods entering and leaving the empire. The taxes brought great wealth to Mali. Mali's trading empire began during the 1300s. That was many years before Christopher Columbus sailed to the Americas in 1492.

Trading Cities

Mali's cities helped the empire become an important crossroads of trade. These cities included Niani, Jenné, Gao, and Timbuktu. Near each city were villages with many workers. Weavers, fishers, blacksmiths, and leather workers brought their goods to the city to sell.

Traders could find much of what they needed in one place. One griot said this about Niani. He said, "If you want salt, . . . if you want gold, . . . if you want cloth, go to Niani, for the Mecca road passes by Niani. If you want fish, go to Niani, for it is there that the fishermen of Moauti and Jenné come to sell their catches. If you want meat, go to Niani, the country of the great hunters, and the land of the ox and the sheep. . . ."

⚡ TextWork

❸ List three examples of craftworkers found near Mali's trading centers.

_____

_____

_____

❹ Underline the sentence that tells why workers from nearby villages made cities good places for trading.

❺ Reread the griot's words about Niani. Circle five products that could be found there.

This painting shows a toy seller in a Mali market.

6 Why did traders travel in caravans?

_____

_____

_____

7 Underline four ways in which camels are adapted to living in the desert.

Camel Caravans Cross Mali

For hundreds of years, camel caravans crossed the Sahara. A **caravan** is a group of traders who travel together. Traveling in groups was safer than traveling alone. Caravans were the best way for traders to carry goods to cities across the empire.

Travel across the desert was not easy. Traders depended on camels to carry their goods. Some caravans had more than 300 camels.

Often called "ships of the desert," camels adapt well to desert living. They can walk in heat 25 miles or more every day. They can also go a long time without eating food or drinking water. They can carry very heavy loads. Their wide feet do not easily sink into the desert sand.

Camel caravans carried goods across the desert to markets in Mali's trading centers.

Goods and Ideas Travel Across Mali

Traders from North Africa carried many goods to trading centers in West Africa. These goods included slabs of salt, cloth, silk, weapons, and horses. Many traders exchanged salt for gold. They also traded for copper, wood, grains, and kola nuts. Then they took these goods back north. There they traded the goods to Europeans.

Traders from the empire of Mali also crossed the Sahara to North Africa. People in the north traded salt for gold that was mined in West Africa. They also traded for swords, glass, paper, books, spices, and other items from Europe and Asia.

Traders also exchanged ideas. Many of the traders were Muslims. Over time, Islam spread across West Africa.

TextWork

8 Underline the products traders from North Africa brought to trading centers in West Africa.

9 Look at the diagram. Circle the item that came from North Africa.

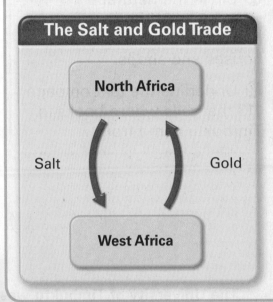

The Salt and Gold Trade

North Africa

Salt   Gold

West Africa

Timbuktu

Timbuktu was an important trading center. It was on the edge of the Sahara and was close to the Niger River. Because it was near both land and water routes, it became a center of trade for the world.

The markets of Timbuktu were busy with traders. Almost every day, caravans reached the city. Some caravans set out to places across Africa. Traders came from places as far away as Italy. Timbuktu and the empire of Mali became well known.

In time, skilled workers from Southwest Asia, Egypt, and other places moved to Timbuktu. They built houses, shops, and other buildings of mud brick. They traded in Timbuktu's markets.

TextWork

10 ⭐ Underline the text that tells what caused Timbuktu to become a center for trade.

11 Circle the natural resources and human resources used to build houses and shops.

12 Underline the text on page 113 that tells where books in Timbuktu came from.

The University of Timbuktu was built in an area of mosques.

When Mansa Musa returned from his pilgrimage, he had workers build a royal palace and mosques in Timbuktu. A **mosque** is a house of worship for Muslims. All were built of mud and wood.

Mansa Musa also had a university built. Its library had books from North Africa and from Greece and Rome. Many teachers, writers, and doctors settled in Timbuktu to be near the library. Many Muslims also came to live and study in Timbuktu. They brought books that held Islamic teachings.

Many of the books in Timbuktu's libraries were beautifully illustrated.

Lesson 4 Review

1. **SUMMARIZE** What effect did trade have on the empire of Mali?

_____

_____

2. Write a description of a **crossroads**.

_____

_____

3. Why did Timbuktu become a center of learning?

_____

_____

4. How did Mali become a wealthy empire?

_____

_____

writing

✎ **Write a Story** Write a story about a journey a trader might make to a trading city in Mali. Include the way the trader travels, the route, the goods to be traded, and what the trading city is like.

An Arabian camel

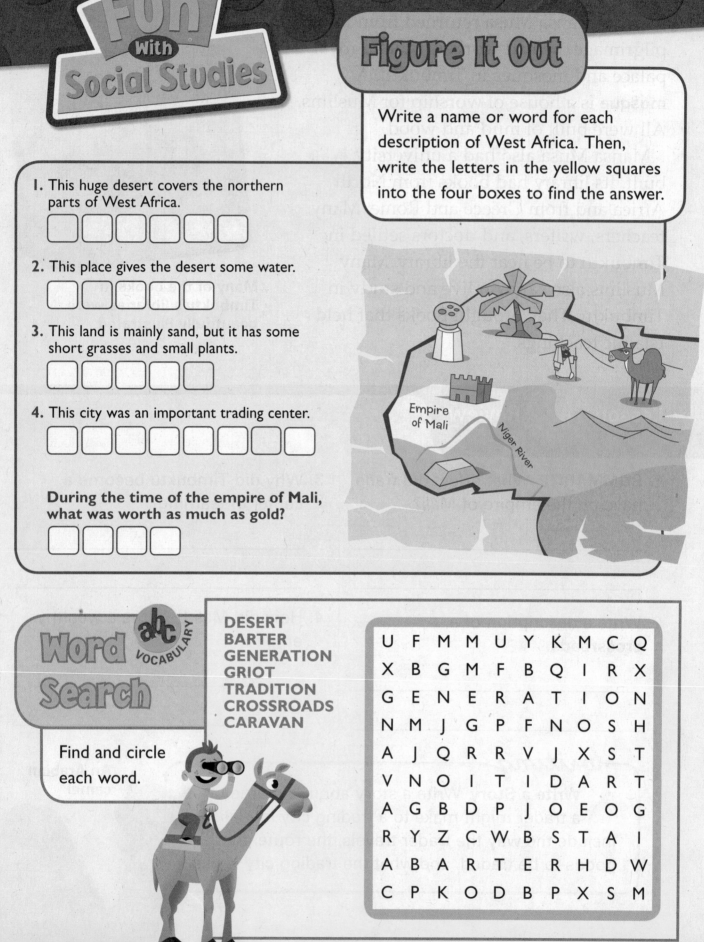

Fun with Social Studies

Figure It Out

Write a name or word for each description of West Africa. Then, write the letters in the yellow squares into the four boxes to find the answer.

1. This huge desert covers the northern parts of West Africa.

☐ ☐ ☐ ☐ ☐ ☐

2. This place gives the desert some water.

☐ ☐ ☐ ☐ ☐

3. This land is mainly sand, but it has some short grasses and small plants.

☐ ☐ ☐ ☐ ☐

4. This city was an important trading center.

☐ ☐ ☐ ☐ ☐ ☐ ☐ ☐ ☐

During the time of the empire of Mali, what was worth as much as gold?

☐ ☐ ☐ ☐

Empire of Mali

Niger River

Word Search

abc VOCABULARY

DESERT
BARTER
GENERATION
GRIOT
TRADITION
CROSSROADS
CARAVAN

Find and circle each word.

U	F	M	M	U	Y	K	M	C	Q
X	B	G	M	F	B	Q	I	R	X
G	E	N	E	R	A	T	I	O	N
N	M	J	G	P	F	N	O	S	H
A	J	Q	R	R	V	J	X	S	T
V	N	O	I	T	I	D	A	R	T
A	G	B	D	P	J	O	E	O	G
R	Y	Z	C	W	B	S	T	A	I
A	B	A	R	T	E	R	H	D	W
C	P	K	O	D	B	P	X	S	M

Terrific Travels

Josie sent postcards from a trip to the empire of Mali. Write what each postcard describes.

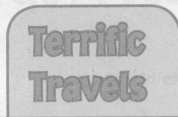

Dear Grandmother,

I visited Timbuktu. There, the King had a library and university built. His name is

_____

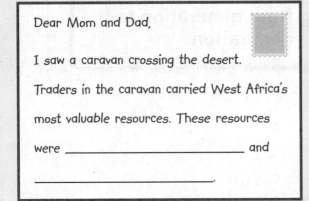

Dear Mom and Dad,

I saw a caravan crossing the desert. Traders in the caravan carried West Africa's most valuable resources. These resources were _____ and

_____

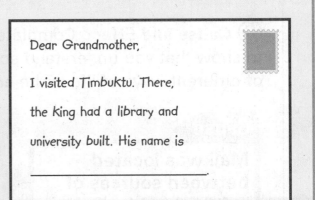

Dear Uncle Pete,

Today, I listened to a storyteller in a market in West Africa. A storyteller in West Africa is called a

_____

Review and Test Prep

The Big Idea

The location of a place can affect its history.

Summarize the Unit

Focus Skill **Cause and Effect** Complete the graphic organizer to show that you understand some causes and effects of different ways of life in the empire of Mali.

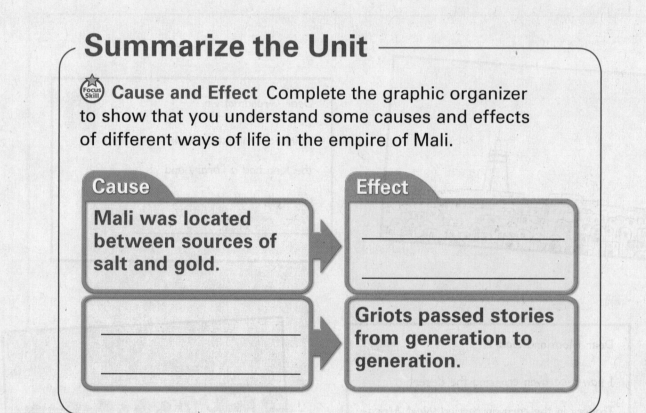

Cause

Mali was located between sources of salt and gold.

Effect

_____

_____

_____

Griots passed stories from generation to generation.

Use Vocabulary

Complete each sentence with a vocabulary term from the Word Bank.

1. In Mali, people grew crops on the _____.

2. Timbuktu was a major _____ of trade because of its resources and location.

3. A _____ extends across the northern part of West Africa.

4. Griots passed on _____ and stories from one generation to the next in Mali.

Word Bank

desert p. 90

savanna p. 92

oasis p. 92

traditions
 p. 103

crossroads
 p. 108

Think About It

Circle the letter of the correct answer.

5.

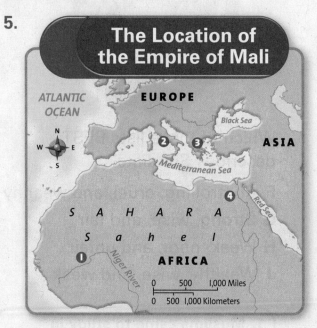

The Location of the Empire of Mali

ATLANTIC OCEAN
EUROPE
Black Sea
ASIA
Mediterranean Sea
❷ ❸
❹
Red Sea
S A H A R A
S a h e l
❶
Niger River
AFRICA

0   500   1,000 Miles
0 500 1,000 Kilometers

Which number shows where the empire of Mali was located?

A 1

B 2

C 3

D 4

6.

- rivers
- mostly dry climate
- gold

These are examples of Mali's—

F human characteristics

G human resources

H physical characteristics

J capital resources

7. The empire of Mali was located in the—

A northern region of Africa

B eastern region of Africa

C western region of Africa

D southern region of Africa

8. Which physical characteristic formed the northern edge of the empire of Mali?

F River

G Sea

H Desert

J Mountain

9. Which are ways the people of Mali changed the land?

A Mining and bartering

B Irrigating and trading

C Trading and farming

D Farming and mining

10. In the empire of Mali, salt was so important it was often traded for—

F iron

G camels

H grains

J gold

11. The people of Mali used salt to—

A find gold

B stay healthy and preserve food

C help crops grow

D use as a food for camels

12. Human characteristics of Mali included—

F oases, deserts, and savannas

G seas, villages, and traders

H farmers, miners, and traders

J millet, beans, and peanuts

13. Tools used for mining salt and gold are examples of—

A capital resources

B human resources

C goods

D services

14.

> Toumani is a storyteller who passes on traditions and stories from one generation to the next. He uses the oral tradition to tell Mali's history.

In these sentences, Toumani is a—

F trader

G griot

H farmer

J king

15. The empire of Mali was ruled by rich and powerful—

A dictators

B presidents

C kings

D griots

16.

Which of these lists BEST describes Sundiata?

F Controlling, cruel, and wealthy

G Strong, wise, and fair

H Weak, poor, and unfair

J Wealthy, wise, and weak

17.

> 1. Muslims came to study in Timbuktu.
> 2. Mansa Musa went on a pilgrimage.
> 3. Mansa Musa became ruler.
> 4. Columbus sailed to North America.

Which is the correct time order for the events in the list?

A 1, 2, 3, 4

B 1, 3, 4, 2

C 3, 2, 1, 4

D 4, 3, 1, 2

18. Which was the BEST way for traders to carry goods?

F Horseback

G Ship

H Wagon

J Camel caravan

19.

Cause		Effect
?	→	Timbuktu was an important trading center.

Which cause replaces the question mark?

A Timbuktu was the capital of the empire of Mali.

B Timbuktu was located near land and water routes.

C Timbuktu had houses made of mud brick.

D Timbuktu had mosques and a university.

20.
- an important city in Mali
- a trading center
- a place where Muslims studied
- the location of a university with books from North Africa, Greece, and Rome

Which of these should be the title of the list above?

F The Routes of the Sahara

G The City of Jenné

H The City of Timbuktu

J The Palace of Sundiata

Answer these questions.

21. How did the location of Mali affect trade?

_____

_____

_____

22. Explain how the people of Mali used human resources and capital resources to get natural resources, such as gold and salt.

_____

_____

_____

23. Why did Mali became a wealthy empire?

_____

_____

_____

A sandstorm! We need to find shelter fast.

Oops! You and Eco have fallen through time. It seems that you are somewhere in the empire of Mali. You can't get back home unless you can persuade a desert trader to let you travel with him from town to town. Go online to play the game now.

Show What You Know

✏️ Writing Write a Journal Entry

Imagine visiting Timbuktu during Mansa Musa's time. Write a journal entry to describe your experience. Describe the city and why it was important. Find and use information from print and non-print sources in your journal entry.

🖌️ Activity Make a Catalog

Make a catalog about the natural, human, and capital resources in the empire of Mali. On one page, list the major natural resources and tell where they were found. Then add a page for each of the three main jobs in the empire. For each job, draw a picture that shows the natural, human, and capital resources used to provide goods and services. Add labels to your drawing.

Exploring the Americas

Early explorers from Europe met different groups of American Indians.

Spotlight on Standards

THE BIG IDEA Over time, many people have explored the world around them.

SOL **HISTORY AND SOCIAL SCIENCE SOL**
3.3a, 3.3b, 3.5c, 3.5d, 3.6

Set the Stage

Study the map. Circle the names of the four explorers from Europe. Then trace the route of the first explorer to sail.

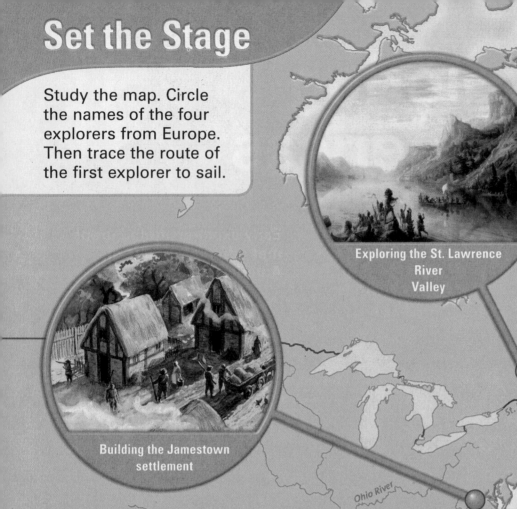

Exploring the St. Lawrence River Valley

Building the Jamestown settlement

Landing near St. Augustine, Florida

Newfoundland Island

St. Lawrence River

ATLANTIC OCEAN

Ohio River

James River

NORTH AMERICA

Mississippi River

Rio Grande

Gulf of Mexico

San Salvador

Cuba

Hispaniola

Puerto Rico

Caribbean Sea

PACIFIC OCEAN

SOUTH AMERICA

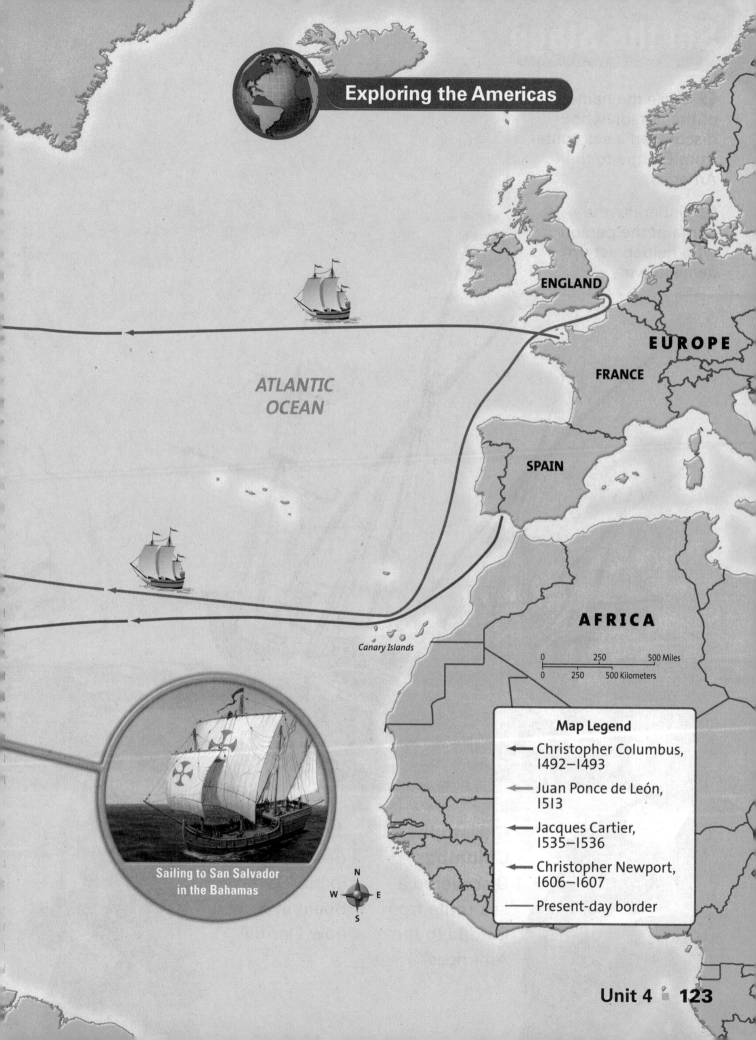

Exploring the Americas

ENGLAND

EUROPE

FRANCE

SPAIN

AFRICA

ATLANTIC
OCEAN

Canary Islands

Sailing to San Salvador
in the Bahamas

0   250   500 Miles
0   250   500 Kilometers

Map Legend

— Christopher Columbus,
1492–1493

— Juan Ponce de León,
1513

— Jacques Cartier,
1535–1536

— Christopher Newport,
1606–1607

— Present-day border

N
W   E
S

Set the Stage

1 Circle the name of the person who discovered a sea route from Europe to the Americas.

2 Underline the name of the person who helped set up Jamestown.

Christopher Columbus
Discovered a sea route from Europe to the Americas

Juan Ponce de León
Explored for Spain in what is now Florida

People from Europe sailed across the Atlantic Ocean to explore.

Jacques Cartier
Explored for France in the St. Lawrence River Valley

Christopher Newport
Helped set up the English settlement of Jamestown

European

A **European** is a person from one of the countries in Europe. p. 130

explorer

An **explorer** is a person who travels seeking new discoveries. p. 130

colony

England set up a colony in Virginia. A **colony** is a settlement ruled by a country that is far away. p. 136

expedition

Explorers went on expeditions. An **expedition** is a trip for a purpose. p. 142

conflict

Settlers sometimes had **conflicts**, or disagreements, in their new communities. p. 143

achievement

An **achievement** is the reaching of a goal through hard work. p. 158

Reading Social Studies

⭐ Focus Skill Compare and Contrast

Learn

Comparing and contrasting can help you understand how things are alike and different. To **compare** things is to tell how they are alike, or similar. *Like, both, all, also, too,* and *similar* are words that compare. To **contrast** things is to tell how they are different. *Different from, unlike, however, but,* and *in a different way* are words and phrases that contrast.

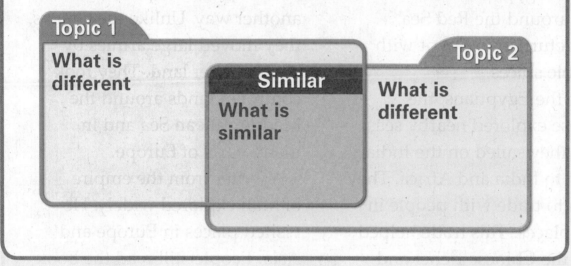

Topic 1
What is different

Similar
What is similar

Topic 2
What is different

Practice

Read the paragraphs. Circle how people in ancient times were alike. Then underline how they were different. The first paragraph has been done for you.

People in ancient times explored, or traveled to discover, new places. However, they explored for different reasons. Many people who explored all hoped to become rich. Some wanted to find land, but others wanted gold.

Similar
Different

Read the following paragraphs. Then complete the activities below.

Exploring in Ancient Times

Exploring new places was important in ancient times. People from ancient Egypt, China, Greece, Rome, and Mali all explored faraway lands.

More than 4,500 years ago, the Egyptians sailed to lands around the Red Sea. They returned to Egypt with valuable spices.

Like the Egyptians, the Chinese explored nearby seas. Later, they sailed on the Indian Ocean to India and Africa. They began to trade with people in these places. This trade helped make the Chinese richer and more powerful.

The Greeks explored an area of the world different from the Chinese. They sailed from the Mediterranean Sea to the Atlantic Ocean. They reached what is now England.

The Romans explored in another way. Unlike the Greeks, they moved large armies by sea and over land. They took control of lands around the Mediterranean Sea and in many parts of Europe.

A writer from the empire of Mali explored widely. He visited places in Europe and Asia. People still read the book he wrote about his travels.

1. **In the first and third paragraphs, underline words that compare.**

2. **In the fourth and fifth paragraphs, circle words that contrast.**

3. **Write a sentence that compares and contrasts the places that these ancient peoples explored.**

_____

_____

About 500 years ago, people from Europe began to explore places unknown to them. One place they set out to explore was the Atlantic Ocean. **Think about why people might have wanted to explore the Atlantic Ocean.**

Today, people visit this early European castle and port in Spain.

Essential Question

✔ What were the different motivations of early European explorers?

HISTORY AND SOCIAL SCIENCE SOL
3.3b

TextWork

1 What is a European?

_____

_____

2 Circle the text that tells two parts of the world that Europeans in the late 1400s did not know existed.

3 Study the map below. Why do you think early Europeans only knew about these parts of the world?

_____

_____

Exploring the World

In the late 1400s, Europeans did not know much about the world. A **European** is a person from one of the countries of Europe. At that time, Europeans did not know how big the world really was. World maps included only Europe, Asia, and part of Africa. Europeans did not know that North America and South America existed.

Exploring the Atlantic Ocean

Spain, France, and England are countries in Europe. Over time, all three countries sent explorers into the unknown waters of the Atlantic Ocean. An **explorer** is a person who travels seeking new discoveries. Exploring an unknown ocean was full of danger, both real and imagined.

A European map of the world from 1489

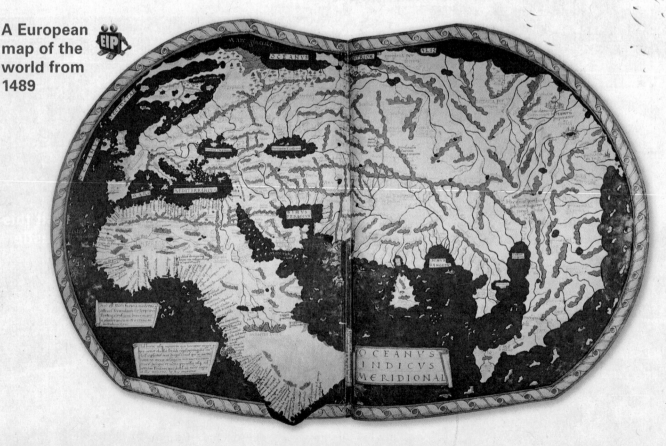

Some explorers believed that giant sea monsters existed.

People with good educations knew that Earth was round. But others thought that if people sailed far from land, they might fall off the edge of the world. Some believed in giant sea monsters. They feared that the monsters might swallow ships.

Reasons for Exploring

Early European explorers had different **motivations**, or reasons, for exploring. Some wanted to gain new lands. Others hoped to find riches, such as gold and silver. Still others wanted to spread their religion to people in other places.

Some explorers hoped to find a western sea route to Asia. Europeans wanted spices and silk from Asia. Traveling east to Asia by land was difficult. Explorers hoped sailing west would be easier.

 **TextWork**

❹ Underline the text that describes the meaning of the word *motivations*.

❺ List four reasons that early Europeans had for exploring.

_____

_____

_____

_____

Children in History

Young Sailors

Many boys sailed with the early European explorers. These young sailors did different jobs on the ships. Most cooked and cleaned. Some served as musicians or as ship artists. A special job was ringing a bell to announce the time.

Make It Relevant Which activities in your daily life are like those of the young sailors?

Lesson 1 Review

1. **SUMMARIZE** What were some different motivations for early European explorers?

_____

_____

_____

2. Which **European** countries sent **explorers** into the Atlantic Ocean?

_____

_____

Circle the letter of the correct answer.

3. European explorers wanted to find a new sea route to Asia to—

   A link sea routes in the east

   B draw better maps of the world

   C discover the world's size

   D have an easier route for trade

An instrument used to sail ships

Write a Report Choose one reason Europeans explored. Find information from print and non-print sources to write a report about the reason.

Columbus Sails the Atlantic

In 1492, Christopher Columbus sailed west across the Atlantic Ocean. He found lands that had been unknown to Europeans before that time. **Think about the results of Christopher Columbus's voyages.**

Replicas of Columbus's ships

Essential Questions

✓ Who were some of the important explorers from Spain, England, and France?

✓ What were the different motivations of these early European explorers?

✓ What were the successes of these early European explorers?

✓ Where is the country of Spain located on a world map?

✓ Where is the region of San Salvador in the Bahamas located on a map?

✓ What were the effects of European explorations on American Indians?

SOL HISTORY AND SOCIAL SCIENCE SOL
3.3a, 3.3b, 3.5c, 3.5d

Sailing West

Christopher Columbus was an Italian sailor. He thought he could reach Asia by sailing west across the Atlantic Ocean. Columbus began planning a voyage, or journey by sea, to find a western sea route.

Finding a Sponsor

Like other explorers, Columbus needed a sponsor for his voyage. A **sponsor** is a person or group who pays for another's activity. Explorers often asked rulers of countries in Europe to be their sponsors.

Columbus asked King Ferdinand and Queen Isabella of Spain to pay for his voyage. In return, Columbus promised to claim land for Spain. To **claim** something means to say that you own it.

TextWork

❶ Underline the reason that Columbus wanted to explore.

❷ (Focus Skill) How was Columbus like other explorers?

_____

_____

_____

❸ Study the painting and caption. Circle the names of the two people meeting with Columbus.

Columbus told his plans for a voyage to King Ferdinand and Queen Isabella of Spain.

Columbus sailed from Spain with three ships— the *Niña*, *Pinta*, and *Santa Maria*.

The First Voyage

Columbus set sail with three ships on August 3, 1492. The voyage was a long and rough one. Finally, on October 12, a sailor called out, "Land, land!"

Columbus was sure he had reached Asia. Instead, he had landed on an island in the Bahamas, off the coast of North America. Even though people already lived there, Columbus named the island San Salvador. He claimed it for Spain.

Columbus explored other islands in the area. On Hispaniola (ees•pah•NYOH•lah), he found colorful parrots, gold, and spices. He also met the Taino (TY•noh) people. The Taino were American Indians. In his journal, Columbus wrote that the Taino were skilled cotton farmers and generous people.

TextWork

4 When did Columbus's voyage begin?

_____

5 (Focus Skill) How was the place where Columbus landed different from the place where he thought he had landed?

_____

_____

_____

_____

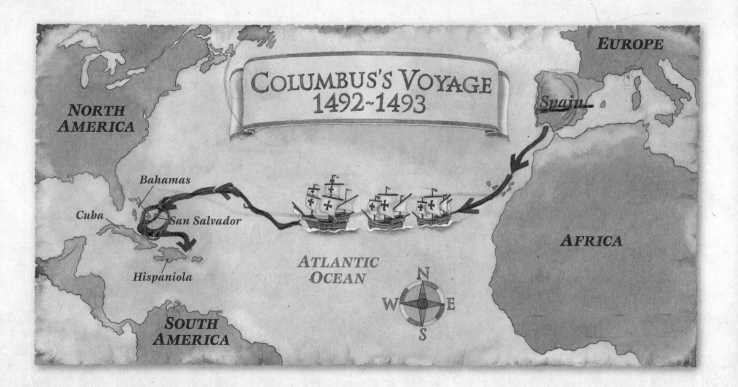

Columbus's Voyage 1492-1493

EUROPE

NORTH AMERICA

Bahamas

Cuba

San Salvador

Hispaniola

SOUTH AMERICA

ATLANTIC OCEAN

Spain

AFRICA

N W E S

Columbus's Successes

After Columbus returned home, Spain's rulers paid him to make three more voyages. They wanted more gold. They also wanted Columbus to set up colonies. A **colony** is a settlement ruled by a country that is far away. Columbus set up a colony for Spain on Hispaniola.

Columbus never found a western sea route to Asia. Even so, he was the first European to discover a sea route to the Americas. The Americas is another name for North America and South America.

Columbus was also the first European of his time to reach places in the Western Hemisphere. His writings gave Europeans important information about these places. Soon other explorers from Europe were sailing to the Americas.

TextWork

6 On the map, trace Columbus's voyage to San Salvador. Underline the name of the European country from which he began his voyage. Circle where San Salvador is located.

7 Did Columbus reach his goals? Explain.

_____

_____

_____

_____

Effects on American Indians

Europeans sometimes called the Western Hemisphere the "New World." It was new to them. However, American Indians had lived there for thousands of years. They had their own ways of life.

The travels of European explorers had a big impact, or effect, on American Indians. American Indians experienced changes in their cultures and environments.

Europeans brought many new things to the Americas. For example, they brought metal tools. Without knowing it, they also brought European diseases. These diseases killed many American Indians.

8 Underline the ___ that tells how lo___ Indians had lived ___ Americas.

9 How did the travels of European explorers affect American Indians?

_____

_____

_____

_____

The arrival of Europeans in the Americas affected American Indians already living there.

1. **SUMMARIZE** Why did Christopher Columbus want to sail west?

_____

_____

_____

2. Write a sentence about Columbus and Spain that includes the word **sponsor**.

_____

_____

_____

3. What were Columbus's successes?

_____

_____

_____

Circle the letter of the correct answer.

4. Where did Columbus first land in the Americas?

   A Hispaniola

   B San Salvador

   C Central America

   D South America

Draw a line connecting each person or group on the left with the correct description on the right.

5. Christopher Columbus

6. Taino

7. king and queen of Spain

lived in the Bahamas for a long time

wanted gold and land for colonies

found a sea route to the Americas

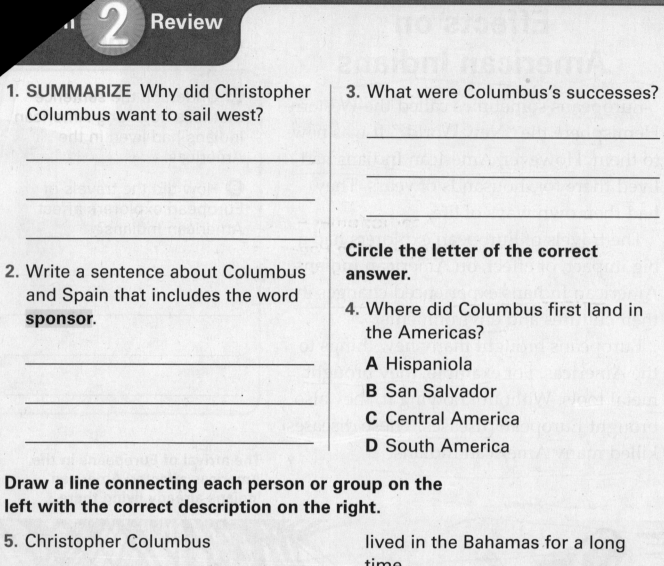

writing

✏ **Write a Journal Entry** Imagine you are on Columbus's first voyage to the Americas. Write a journal entry about the group's goals. Then tell about what you saw and did. Tell how the trip affected the American Indians you met.

A Spanish stamp

Ponce de León Explores Florida

Spain was the sponsor for other explorers who sailed to the Americas. One was Juan Ponce de León (HWAHN POHN•say day lay•OHN). Ponce de León was a Spanish soldier. **Think about why Ponce de León might have explored new lands.**

The Atlantic coast near
St. Augustine, Florida

Essential Questions

✔ Who were some of the important explorers from Spain, England, and France?

✔ What were the different motivations of these early European explorers?

✔ What were the successes of these early European explorers?

✔ Where is the region of St. Augustine, Florida, located on a map?

✔ What were the effects of European explorations on American Indians?

SOL **HISTORY AND SOCIAL SCIENCE SOL**
3.3a, 3.3b, 3.5c, 3.5d

Ponce de León

Spain's rulers asked Juan Ponce de León to find riches in the Americas. They also asked him to conquer, or take control of, more lands there.

Arriving in the Americas

In 1493, Ponce de León sailed with Christopher Columbus on his second voyage. On Hispaniola, he led Spanish soldiers against the Taino. He forced the Taino to mine gold and work on farms.

Later, Ponce de León set up a Spanish colony on what is now Puerto Rico. The king of Spain rewarded him. He named Ponce de León as ruler of Puerto Rico. Ponce de León became very rich.

On Puerto Rico, Ponce de León forced the Taino to mine gold. Many died from the hard work and European diseases.

❶ Underline two reasons why Spain wanted Ponce de León to explore.

❷ (Focus Skill) What experience did Ponce de León and Columbus share?

_In 1493 ?_
Ponce de Leon s
_____

❸ How did Ponce de León treat the American Indians?

_____
_____
_____

A statue of Ponce de León

The Fountain of Youth

Ponce de León takes water he believes is from the Fountain of Youth.

While in Puerto Rico, Ponce de León heard the legend of the Fountain of Youth. A **legend** is a story that may or may not be true. The legend said the fountain's water could make old people young again.

In Search of a Legend

Spain wanted Ponce de León to look for more riches and land. He decided to look for the Fountain of Youth at the same time. The legend said the fountain was on an island in the Bahamas. In 1513, Ponce de León set out to find it.

In time, Ponce de León reached what he thought was the island. He named the land Florida, which means "full of flowers" in Spanish. Ponce de León had landed near the location of the present-day city of St. Augustine in northern Florida.

Ponce de León set up a Spanish colony on Puerto Rico. Today, Puerto Rico is part of the United States.

4 (Focus Skill) How was the place where Ponce de León landed different from the place where he thought he had landed?

He Did not land on the Bahamas.

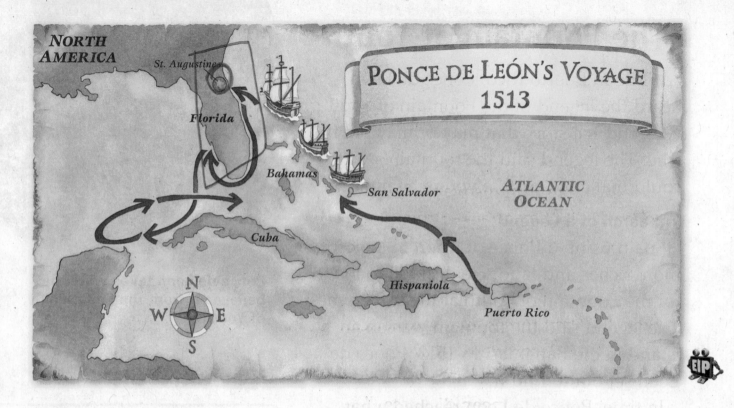

PONCE DE LEÓN'S VOYAGE
1513

NORTH AMERICA
St. Augustine
Florida
Bahamas
San Salvador
ATLANTIC OCEAN
Cuba
Hispaniola
Puerto Rico

Exploring Florida

Ponce de León never found the Fountain of Youth. He did have two successes, however. He was the first European to set foot in what is now Florida. He also claimed Florida for Spain. This land would later become part of the United States.

Colonies Fail

Ponce de León explored Florida's east coast. Then he explored part of its west coast before returning to Puerto Rico.

Later, the king of Spain asked Ponce de León to start a colony in Florida. In 1521, Ponce de León led an expedition to Florida. An **expedition** is a trip for a purpose. Ponce de León sailed to Florida with two ships. The ships carried about 200 settlers.

TextWork

❺ Study the map. Circle St. Augustine. Then draw a box around the area where Ponce de León landed.

❻ Underline Ponce de León's two successes.

❼ What was the purpose of Ponce de León's expedition to Florida in 1521?

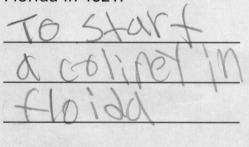
To start a coliney in floida

Conflicts with American Indians

Ponce de León and the settlers landed on Florida's west coast. Conflicts soon broke out between the settlers and the American Indians there. A **conflict** is a disagreement between people.

The American Indians wanted to protect their lands, so they attacked the settlers. Ponce de León was hit by a poisonous arrow. He later died from his injury.

Over time, more Spanish settlers arrived in Florida. They forced many American Indians to work for them. Many of the American Indians died from the hard work and from European diseases.

American Indians fought to keep their lands. However, they had only bows and arrows. The Spanish brought horses and guns. They used these to force the American Indians off their lands.

TextWork

8 Underline the sentence that explains what the American Indians wanted to protect by attacking settlers.

9 (Focus Skill) How were the weapons of the American Indians and the Spanish different?

Indians had bows and arrows settelers had Horses and guns

10 Study the illustration. List three jobs people are doing.

cooking ship building basket fishing fishing

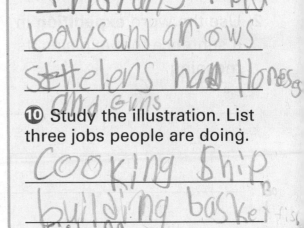

Early American Indians in what is now Florida lived in villages.

1. **SUMMARIZE** What were Ponce de León's successes?

_____

_____

_____

2. Use the word **expedition** in a sentence that explains its meaning.

_____

_____

_____

3. What conflicts did Ponce de León have with American Indians?

_____

_____

Circle the letter of the correct answer.

4. In 1513, Ponce de León searched for more riches and land for Spain and for—

   A the Fountain of Youth

   B a western route to Asia

   C an eastern route to Asia

   D other European settlements

Draw a line connecting each place on the left with the correct description on the right.

5. Puerto Rico

6. St. Augustine

7. Florida

land named by Ponce de León

land ruled by Ponce de León

a present-day city in northern Florida

A Spanish coin

writing

🖎 **Write a Poem** Ponce de León looked for the legendary Fountain of Youth. Write a poem about this voyage. Tell whether he found what he was looking for.

Cartier Explores Farther North

The French watched as Spain sent explorers to the Americas. France decided that it should pay for an expedition, too. France's king chose the French explorer Jacques Cartier (ZHAHK kar•TYAY) to be its leader. **Think about why the French might have wanted to explore North America.**

Cartier explored the St. Lawrence River Valley in what is now Canada.

Essential Questions

✓ Who were some of the important explorers from Spain, England, and France?
✓ What were the different motivations of these early European explorers?
✓ What were the successes of these early European explorers?
✓ Where is the region of Québec, Canada, located on a map?
✓ What were the effects of European explorations on American Indians?

HISTORY AND SOCIAL SCIENCE SOL
3.3a, 3.3b, 3.5c, 3.5d

European explorers searched for the Northwest Passage.

TextWork

1 Why did France's king want to send an expedition to North America?

_____

_____

_____

_____

2 (Focus Skill) Underline the sentences that explain how Columbus's belief about North America and Asia differed from that of later explorers.

A French Expedition

The king of France had good reasons for sending an expedition to North America. Like the Spanish, he wanted to gain land and riches. He also hoped to find a water route to Asia. Later, the king would want to start colonies in North America.

The Northwest Passage

Christopher Columbus had believed that North America was part of Asia. Later explorers found out that the two continents were separate. The French hoped to find a water route through or around North America to Asia. This Northwest Passage would make it easier to get spices and other riches back to France.

The St. Lawrence River

In 1534, the king of France chose Jacques Cartier to sail to North America. On his first voyage, Cartier sailed past what is now Newfoundland, a part of Canada. He landed near the mouth of the St. Lawrence River. He claimed the land for France and then explored the area.

Along the way, Cartier met American Indians known as the Iroquois (IR•uh•kwoy). They gave Cartier corn. He had never seen corn before. Cartier took the corn with him back to France. He also brought along two Iroquois.

Cartier had made France's first land claim in North America. He hoped to make a second voyage. Cartier told the king that he could find more land and riches. His story worked.

TextWork

❸ Underline the sentence that tells where Cartier landed in North America.

❹ Circle the new food that the Iroquois gave Cartier.

❺ How do you think the French responded when they first saw American Indians?

_____

_____

_____

_____

"We went along, and about a mile and a halfe [half] farther, we began to finde [find] goodly and large fieldes [fields], full of such corne [corn]."

Jacques Cartier

Cartier took corn back to France.

Québec and Montreal

TextWork

6 What area did Cartier explore after returning to North America in 1535?

_____

_____

7 Study the map. Trace the route of Cartier's voyage. Circle the region where the city of Québec is located.

8 Underline the sentence that explains why Cartier went on a third voyage.

In 1535, Cartier returned to North America. He explored the St. Lawrence River Valley in Canada. He also set up a camp near what is now the city of Québec.

A Colony Fails

Cartier left Québec and sailed west on the St. Lawrence River. He reached an American Indian community near a high hill. This site would later become the city of Montreal. Rapids stopped Cartier from going farther west on the river. **Rapids** are shallow, rocky areas of fast-moving water.

Cartier made a third voyage to North America in 1541. He went to **colonize**, or set up a colony in, Canada. The colony failed, and Cartier returned to France. He never again returned to North America.

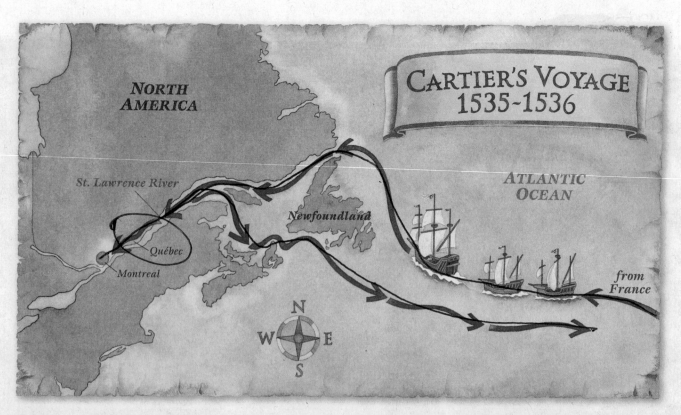

NORTH AMERICA

CARTIER'S VOYAGE 1535~1536

ATLANTIC OCEAN

St. Lawrence River

Newfoundland

Québec

Montreal

from France

N W E S

The French and American Indians had mostly good relations.

Cartier's Successes

Cartier never found the Northwest Passage. However, he did have two major successes. Cartier claimed land for France in North America. He also explored the St. Lawrence River Valley.

American Indians and the Fur Trade

Cartier wrote about his travels. In France, fur trappers and traders read his descriptions of the many beavers and other animals found in North America. The French began to trade with American Indians. The French traded tools and other goods for furs. They made a lot of money.

Often French fur trappers lived among the American Indians. They learned their languages and cultures. This helped them develop friendships for trading success.

TextWork

9 Scan the text on this page. Underline Cartier's two major successes.

10 (Focus Skill) How were the relations the French had with American Indians different from those the Spanish had?

_____

_____

_____

_____

1. **SUMMARIZE** Why did France send Jacques Cartier to North America?

_____

_____

_____

_____

2. How did **rapids** on the St. Lawrence River affect Cartier?

_____

_____

_____

3. How did the French and American Indians cooperate?

_____

_____

_____

Circle the letter of the correct answer.

4. What region of North America did Cartier explore?

   A Mississippi River Valley

   B St. Lawrence River Valley

   C Florida

   D Hispaniola

Draw a line connecting each place on the left with the correct description on the right.

5. St. Lawrence River Valley

6. Northwest Passage

7. France

Cartier's sponsor

location of Québec and Montreal

a northern water route that was thought to go to Asia

A beaver hat

activity

🖊 **Create an Advertisement** Suppose you are trying to encourage traders to come to North America. Write an advertisement and use pictures to attract them to the areas that Cartier claimed for France.

Newport Explores Virginia

Spain and France had both claimed land in North America. England also decided to send explorers there. Christopher Newport explored the area that is now Virginia. **Think about how Christopher Newport's voyage might lead to new settlements.**

A replica of one of Newport's early ships

Essential Questions

✓ Who were some of the important European explorers from Spain, England, and France?

✓ What were the different motivations of these early European explorers?

✓ What were the successes of these early European explorers?

✓ Where is the region of Jamestown, Virginia, located on a map?

✓ What were the effects of European explorations on American Indians?

HISTORY AND SOCIAL SCIENCE SOL
3.3a, 3.3b, 3.5c, 3.5d

England's Queen Elizabeth I was a sponsor of early voyages to North America.

The English in North America

Like the French, England's rulers hoped to find a western route to Asia. They also wanted to start a colony in North America. They wanted settlers there to send raw materials and other riches back to England. A **raw material** is a natural resource, such as wood, that can be used to make goods.

Early Expeditions

Queen Elizabeth I approved several early expeditions. In 1583, one explored the Atlantic coast, including what is now Virginia. Later, settlers made two attempts to colonize Roanoke Island in what is now North Carolina. The first group soon ran out of food and returned to England. The second group disappeared.

Founding Jamestown

By 1605, King James I ruled England. He wanted to try again to start a colony in North America. He chose a sailor named Christopher Newport to lead the voyage.

First English Settlement

In December 1606, Newport sailed from England. He left with about 100 men and boys on three ships—the *Susan Constant*, the *Godspeed*, and the *Discovery*. Four months later, the group reached what is now Virginia. They sailed up a wide river. Newport named the river the James River to honor the king.

In May, the settlers chose a site along the James River to build a settlement. Newport named the site Jamestown. Jamestown became the first **permanent**, or long-lasting, English settlement in North America.

TextWork

❸ Underline the name of the person who led the voyage to colonize North America for England.

❹ Study the map and Newport's route. Circle the labels for Jamestown and the James River.

❺ Why do you think it would be important to settle along a river?

To put out lines to grow crops

NORTH AMERICA

Jamestown

Chesapeake Bay

FALL LINE

James River

NEWPORT'S VOYAGE 1606-1607

6 How did the Fall Line keep Newport from sailing west of what is now Richmond?

_____

_____

7 Underline the sentences that tell the mistakes many of the first settlers at Jamestown made.

Jamestown Settlement

Newport explored the James River, searching for a water route through North America. He reached the Fall Line near what is now Richmond. Along the **Fall Line**, the height of land changes suddenly. This change causes rivers to form rapids or waterfalls. The Fall Line of the James River kept Newport from sailing farther west.

A Hard Life

At Jamestown, the first settlers faced terrible hardships. Many did not realize the hard work needed to start a colony. They did not know how to farm and did not want to learn. They just wanted to look for gold and return home rich.

Newport helped Jamestown succeed. The English then settled other parts of Virginia.

In times of peace, the settlers traded with the Powhatan (pow•uh•TAN) and other nearby American Indians for food. Still, many settlers died from hunger and diseases. In times of conflict, other settlers died fighting American Indians. The Indians wanted to protect their lands and stop further settlement.

A Successful Settlement

Newport made four more voyages to Jamestown. On each trip, he brought more supplies and settlers, including women. In time, Jamestown became successful.

Newport did not discover riches or a western route to Asia. However, he did set up Jamestown and bring more settlers. He was also the first European to reach the Fall Line of the James River.

TextWork

8 Underline the sentences that tell about Newport's successes.

9 The English continued to settle Virginia. How do you think this affected the American Indians there?

_____

_____

_____

_____

Temperance Flowerdew

Temperance Flowerdew survived a hurricane at sea on her way to Jamestown. Her first winter there was a time of hardship, and many settlers died. After the winter, Flowerdew married and started a family. Her loyalty to Jamestown helped it survive.

Time

1585 Born   **1628** Died

1609 Flowerdew arrives in Jamestown

1613 Flowerdew marries

Lesson 5 Review

1. **SUMMARIZE** Why did England want to start a colony in North America?

_____

_____

2. Write a sentence about the first **permanent** English settlement in North America.

_____

_____

Circle the letter of the correct answer.

3. Christopher Newport was the first European to—

   A find a sea route to the Americas

   B land in Florida

   C explore the St. Lawrence River

   D reach the Fall Line of the James River

A pitcher from early Jamestown

activity

Draw a Map Make an outline map of Virginia. Label in red the places that Newport explored. Then label in blue the place where you live.

Comparing the Explorers

A statue of Columbus meeting with Spain's rulers

Spain, France, and England all sent explorers to the Americas. Their explorations of the Americas were alike in some ways and different in others. **Think about ways to compare early European explorations of the Americas.**

Essential Questions

✓ Who were some of the important European explorers from Spain, England, and France?

✓ What were the different motivations of these early European explorers?

✓ What were the successes of these early European explorers?

✓ What visual aids are used to gather and classify information?

✓ What were the effects of European explorations on American Indians?

SOL **HISTORY AND SOCIAL SCIENCE SOL**
3.3a, 3.3b, 3.6

TextWork

1 Write an example of a visual aid.

_____

2 Study the table on page 159. Circle the names of the explorers for whom Spain was the sponsor. Underline the name of the area that Jacques Cartier explored. Draw a box around the achievements of Christopher Newport.

3 (Focus Skill) Use the table to describe how the achievements of Juan Ponce de León and Jacques Cartier were alike.

_____

_____

_____

Early Explorations of the Americas

In this unit, you read about some early European explorers of North America. Visual aids can help you better understand and remember what you read. A table is an example of a visual aid.

Using Tables

A table is a useful way to show a lot of information. To make a table, you first gather information. Then you classify the information into categories.

The table on page 159 can help you review the information in this unit. It has four rows and five columns. Rows go across, and columns go up and down. There is one row for each early European explorer. The columns are labeled _Explorer, Sponsor, Reasons for Exploring, Area Explored_, and _Achievements_. An **achievement** is the reaching of a goal through hard work.

A European map of the Americas from 1572

Early European Explorers

Explorer	Sponsor	Reasons for Exploring	Area Explored	Achievements
Christopher Columbus	Spain	• to find a western sea route to Asia • to find gold • to claim land	San Salvador in the Bahamas and nearby islands	• first European to discover a sea route to the Americas • first European of his time to reach places in the Western Hemisphere
Juan Ponce de León	Spain	• to find riches • to claim land	Florida, near St. Augustine, and other parts of Florida's coast	• first European to land in Florida • claimed Florida for Spain
Jacques Cartier	France	• to set up colonies • to find riches • to search for the Northwest Passage	St. Lawrence River Valley near Québec, Canada	• claimed land for France in North America
Christopher Newport	England	• to find riches • to find a western route to Asia • to set up colonies in Virginia	Jamestown, Virginia and the James River	• helped set up Jamestown • made four more voyages to Jamestown • first European to reach the Fall Line of the James River

English gold coins from the 1500s

American Indians were often forced to move as European settlements spread.

Impacts on American Indians

European explorations affected American Indians in many ways. Through trade, American Indians received new kinds of tools and other European goods. However, many Indians also died from diseases that Europeans brought to the Americas. Others died in conflicts with Europeans.

Loss of Homelands

Over time, American Indians lost nearly all of their lands. Explorers claimed the lands for their sponsors. Then other Europeans arrived to settle it. As European settlements spread, American Indians had to move to new places. This meant that they had to adapt to new environments and often change their ways of living.

TextWork

④ Underline the sentences that describe how American Indians died from contact with Europeans.

⑤ What effect did the spread of European settlements have on American Indians?

_____

_____

_____

_____

1. **SUMMARIZE** How can a visual aid, such as a table, help you compare information about early European explorations of North America?

_____

_____

_____

2. Write a sentence about a major **achievement** of one explorer.

_____

_____

_____

3. How were the explorations of Columbus and Ponce de León alike and how were they different?

_____

_____

_____

4. How might moving to new places have been difficult for American Indians who lost their homelands?

_____

_____

_____

Draw a line connecting each sponsor on the left with the correct explorer or explorers on the right.

5. Spain   Christopher Newport

6. France   Jacques Cartier

7. England   Christopher Columbus and Juan Ponce de León

activity

🖌 **Make a Table** Make a table about the accomplishments, or achievements, of each explorer. Use one row for each explorer. Then label two columns *Explorer* and *Accomplishments*. Give your table a title.

English gold coin

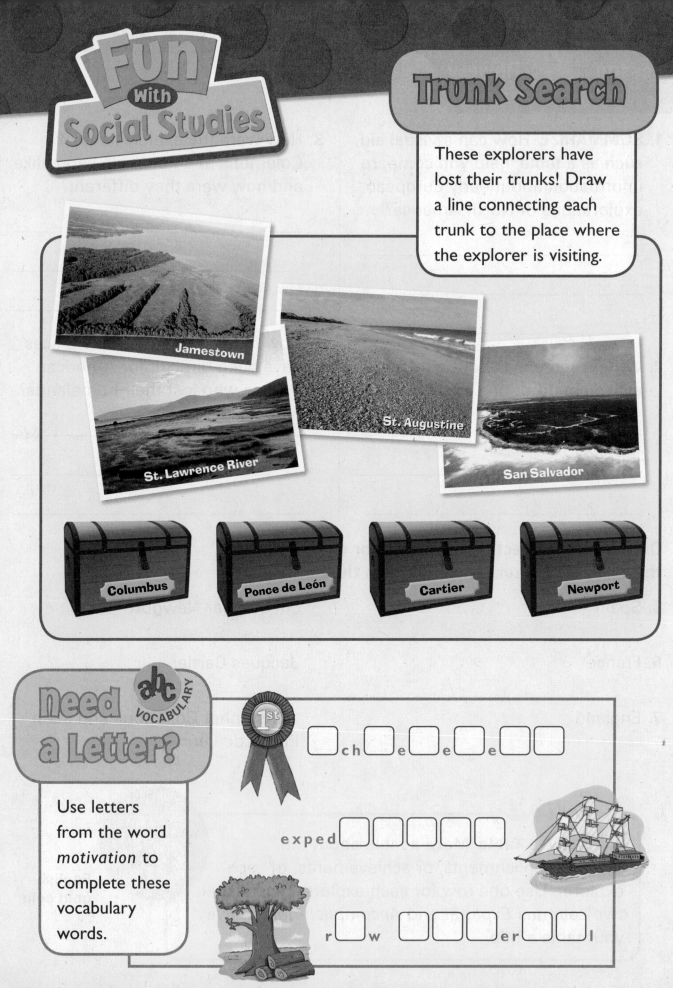

Fun With Social Studies

Trunk Search

These explorers have lost their trunks! Draw a line connecting each trunk to the place where the explorer is visiting.

Jamestown

St. Augustine

St. Lawrence River

San Salvador

Columbus

Ponce de León

Cartier

Newport

Need a Letter?
abc VOCABULARY

Use letters from the word *motivation* to complete these vocabulary words.

1st

☐ c h ☐ e ☐ e ☐ e ☐ ☐

e x p e d ☐ ☐ ☐ ☐ ☐

r ☐ w ☐ ☐ ☐ e r ☐ ☐ l

Who's the Author?

The explorers wrote books about their travels. Write the name of the author below each book.

A Sea Route to America

CLAIMING FLORIDA FOR SPAIN

The St. Lawrence River Valley

The Founding of Jamestown

_____   _____   _____   _____

Map Match

Write the country name for each puzzle piece. Then, write the letter of each country at its location on the map.

A _____

B _____

C _____

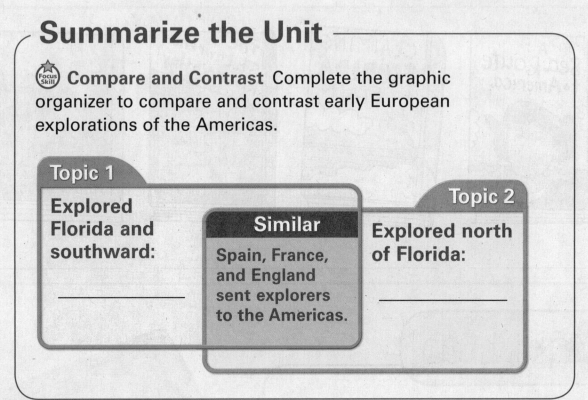

Review and Test Prep

The Big Idea

Over time, many people have explored the world around them.

Summarize the Unit

Focus Skill **Compare and Contrast** Complete the graphic organizer to compare and contrast early European explorations of the Americas.

Topic 1

Explored Florida and southward:

_____

Similar

Spain, France, and England sent explorers to the Americas.

Topic 2

Explored north of Florida:

_____

Use Vocabulary

Complete each sentence with a vocabulary term from the Word Bank.

1. England sent Christopher Newport on an

   _____ to North America.

2. People from Spain, France, and England are

   _____.

3. American Indians and explorers had _____ over land.

4. The early European _____ had sponsors.

Word Bank

Europeans
  p. 130

explorers p. 130

expedition
  p. 142

conflicts p. 143

achievement
  p. 158

Think About It

Circle the letter of the correct answer.

5.

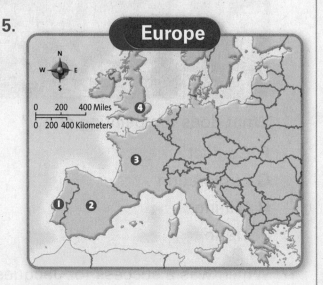

Europe

Which number shows the location of England?

A 1

B 2

C 3

D 4

6. Christopher Columbus first sailed across the Atlantic Ocean to find a sea route to—

F Asia

G Africa

H Australia

J Antarctica

7. Which country was the sponsor for Christopher Columbus?

A Portugal

B Spain

C France

D England

8. Where did Christopher Columbus first land?

F Near St. Augustine, in Florida

G Near Quebéc, in Canada

H At San Salvador, in the Bahamas

J At Jamestown, in Virginia

9. Christopher Columbus found—

A land for Spain in Quebéc

B the Fountain of Youth

C the Northwest Passage

D a sea route to the Americas

10.

1. The Taino Indians were skilled cotton farmers.
2. People knew little about the world in the late 1400s.
3. American Indians lived in towns.
4. Europeans brought deadly diseases to the Americas.

Which sentence describes an effect that Europeans had on American Indians?

F 1

G 2

H 3

J 4

11. Which country was Juan Ponce de León's sponsor?

A Portugal

B Spain

C France

D England

12. Juan Ponce de León explored the Americas to—

    F find riches and conquer land

    G search for the Northwest Passage

    H stop the Taino from mining gold

    J start colonies in Virginia

13.

> A legend said that the Fountain of Youth was on an island in the Bahamas. Ponce de León thought he had landed there.

Where did Juan Ponce de León land?

    A At San Salvador, in the Bahamas

    B At Jamestown, in Virginia

    C Near St. Augustine, in Florida

    D Near Quebéc, in Canada

14. Juan Ponce de León became the first European to reach and claim what is now—

    F Hispaniola

    G Puerto Rico

    H Florida

    J Virginia

15. Which area did France send Jacques Cartier to explore?

    A South America

    B North America

    C Africa

    D Asia

16.

What does the painting show?

    F Conflict

    G Exploration

    H Mining

    J Trade

17. Which was a success for Jacques Cartier?

    A Explored the Mississippi River

    B Colonized North America

    C Claimed land for France in North America

    D Reached what is now Florida

18.

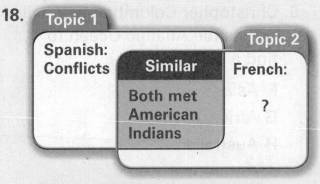

Which difference replaces the question mark?

    F Conflicts

    G No relations

    H Friendly

    J Little contact

19. Which country was the sponsor for Christopher Newport?

    A Portugal

    B Spain

    C France

    D England

20. One reason that Christopher Newport sailed to North America was to—

    F colonize Virginia

    G conquer American Indians

    H claim land in the Bahamas

    J explore Florida

21.

> 1. Newport made four more trips to Jamestown.
> 2. Jamestown became successful.
> 3. Newport arrived at present-day Jamestown.
> 4. Newport reached the Fall Line.

What is the correct order for the list?

    A 1, 2, 3, 4

    B 2, 3, 4, 1

    C 3, 4, 1, 2

    D 4, 1, 2, 3

Answer these questions.

22. What were two different motivations that Europeans had for exploring new lands?

_____

_____

23. What were two successes of Christopher Columbus?

_____

_____

24. How did European settlement in the Americas affect American Indians already living there?

_____

_____

_____

This trip to the Time Museum includes more than just dusty exhibits. If you and Eco can help the curator get the museum ready for opening day, you could earn the chance for a ride on the Time Ship! Go online to play the game now.

HMH

ECO

Show What You Know

✏️ Writing Write a Report

Review information from this unit about the relationship between an explorer and American Indians. Decide which information from the text, pictures, and captions is important to understanding the relationship. Then write a report that descibes whether the relationship was friendly or not friendly and why.

🖌️ Activity Make a Poster

Make a poster about one explorer from this unit. Draw a picture of the explorer and a scene from his voyage. Include a table about the voyage with the following columns: *Year, Sponsor, Goal, Places Explored, Results.* Give your poster a title, and display it in your classroom.

The World Around Us

Spotlight on Standards

THE BIG IDEA People in different locations use their resources and trade with others to meet their needs.

 HISTORY AND SOCIAL SCIENCE SOL
3.4b, 3.4c, 3.5a, 3.5b, 3.5c, 3.5d, 3.5e, 3.6, 3.7, 3.8, 3.9

Earth as seen from space

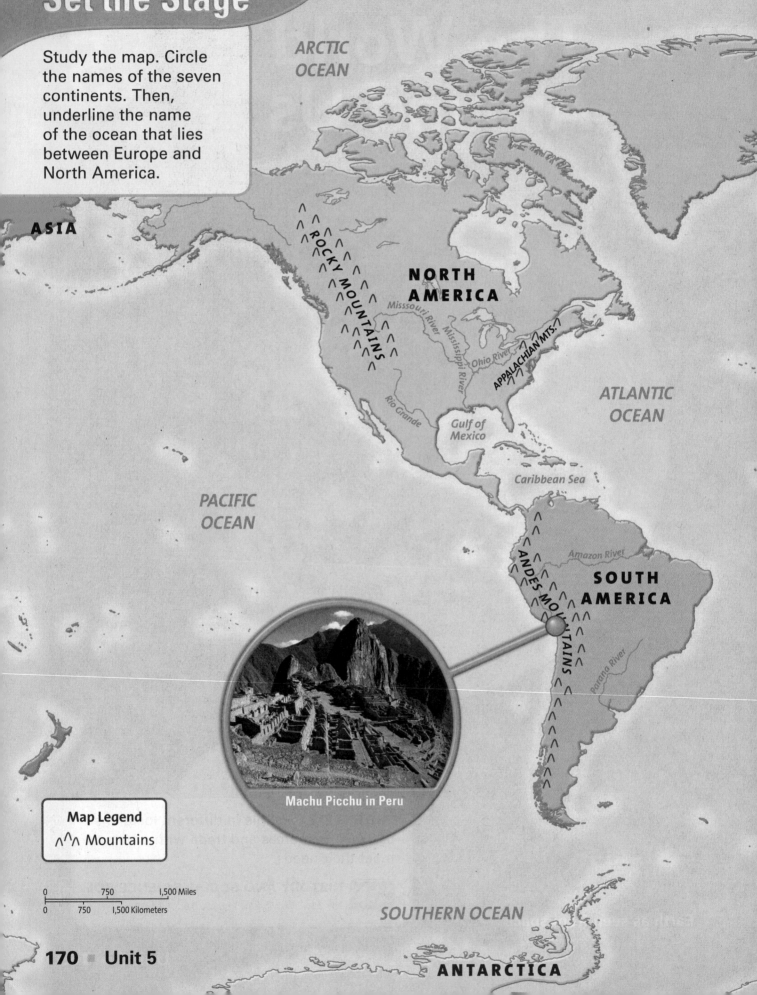

Set the Stage

Study the map. Circle the names of the seven continents. Then, underline the name of the ocean that lies between Europe and North America.

ARCTIC OCEAN

ASIA

ROCKY MOUNTAINS

NORTH AMERICA

Misssouri River

Mississippi River

Ohio River

APPALACHIAN MTS.

Rio Grande

Gulf of Mexico

ATLANTIC OCEAN

Caribbean Sea

PACIFIC OCEAN

ANDES MOUNTAINS

Amazon River

SOUTH AMERICA

Parana River

Machu Picchu in Peru

Map Legend

∧∧∧ Mountains

| 0 | 750 | 1,500 Miles |
| 0 | 750 | 1,500 Kilometers |

SOUTHERN OCEAN

ANTARCTICA

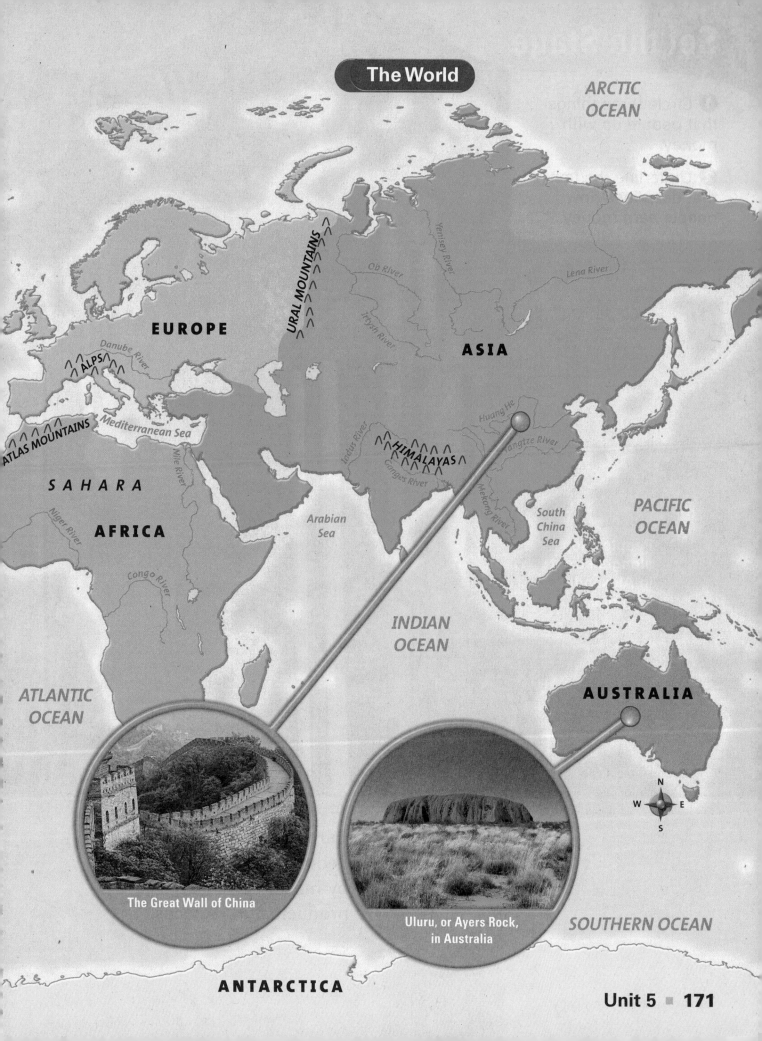

The World

ARCTIC OCEAN

URAL MOUNTAINS

EUROPE

ASIA

ALPS

Danube River

ATLAS MOUNTAINS

Mediterranean Sea

Ob River

Yenisey River

Lena River

Irtysh River

Indus River

HIMALAYAS

Ganges River

Huang He

Yangtze River

Mekong River

SAHARA

Nile River

Arabian Sea

South China Sea

PACIFIC OCEAN

AFRICA

Niger River

Congo River

INDIAN OCEAN

ATLANTIC OCEAN

AUSTRALIA

The Great Wall of China

Uluru, or Ayers Rock, in Australia

SOUTHERN OCEAN

N
W E
S

ANTARCTICA

Set the Stage

1 Circle three things that people do with money.

2 Underline the text that describes how people earn money.

People shop along a street in Alexandria, Virginia.

Earn Money
People earn money by making or selling products and services.

GALLERIE MICHELE
Fine Art
Unique Gifts
Decorative Art

BUGSY'S
UPSTAIRS

POP'S

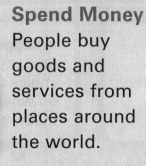

Spend Money
People buy goods and services from places around the world.

Save Money
It is important to make good choices about using your money.

SAVINGS ACCOUNT
$
BANK BOOK

Preview Vocabulary

region

The United States is divided into five **regions**, or places with common characteristics. p. 179

hemisphere

Earth is shaped like a sphere, or ball. Half of a sphere is called a **hemisphere**. p. 180

equator

The **equator** divides Earth into the Northern and Southern Hemispheres. p. 180

prime meridian

The **prime meridian** divides Earth into the Eastern and Western Hemispheres. p. 181

economic choice

People make an **economic choice** when they choose what they want to buy. p. 204

opportunity cost

An **opportunity cost** is the next best choice that is given up when a decision is made. p. 206

Reading Social Studies

Focus Skill: Draw Conclusions

Learn

A **conclusion** is a general statement about an idea. To draw a conclusion, you use evidence, or what you learn from reading. You also use knowledge, or what you know.

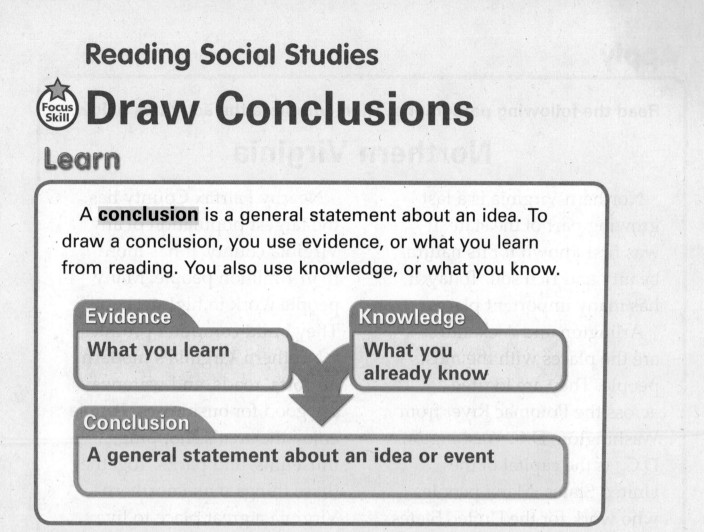

Evidence
What you learn

Knowledge
What you already know

Conclusion
A general statement about an idea or event

Practice

Draw a conclusion for each paragraph. The first paragraph has been done for you.

High-tech, or high technology, businesses make computer products. People use computers at home, at work, and at school.   **Evidence** / **Knowledge**

Conclusion: High-tech businesses are important.   **Conclusion**

Many Virginians work at high-tech jobs making computers. These workers need special training and skills.

Conclusion: _____

_____

Apply

Read the following paragraphs. Then complete the activities below.

Northern Virginia

Northern Virginia is a fast-growing part of the state. It was first known for its natural beauty and rich soil. Today, it has many important places.

Arlington and Alexandria are the places with the most people. They are located across the Potomac River from Washington, D.C. Washington, D.C., is the capital of the United States. Many people who work for the United States government live in northern Virginia.

Nearby Fairfax County has the largest population of any Virginia county. It has more than 1 million people. Many people work in high-tech jobs. They build computer products.

Northern Virginia's modern airports, roads, and waterways are good for businesses. People enjoy the area's shopping, museums, and parks. Together, these things make northern Virginia a great place to live. Experts say that the area will continue to grow.

1. **What knowledge did you have about northern Virginia before reading the article?**

2. **Underline the evidence in the second paragraph that supports the conclusion that many people who work for the United States government live in northern Virginia.**

3. **Read the last paragraph again. What conclusion can you draw about the future of northern Virginia?**

Looking at Places on Earth

You have read about many places on Earth. You can use maps and globes to show the location of these places. Maps and globes are geographic (jee•uh•GRA•fik) tools. They tell you more about what a place might look like. **Think about what maps and globes can show people about places.**

An outdoor globe near New York City

Essential Questions
✓ Where are the seven continents and the five oceans located on a world map?
✓ What imaginary lines are used to create hemispheres?
✓ What are the names of the four hemispheres?
✓ On which continents are England, Spain, France, and the United States located?
✓ Where are the countries of Spain, England, and France located on a world map?
✓ Where are the regions (general areas) of San Salvador in the Bahamas; St. Augustine, Florida; Québec, Canada; and Jamestown, Virginia located on a map?

SOL HISTORY AND SOCIAL SCIENCE SOL
3.5a, 3.5b, 3.5c, 3.5d, 3.6

 **TextWork**

1 Skim this page to find a sentence that lists the names of all seven continents. Underline that sentence.

2 On the map, circle each continent's name.

3 On the map, draw a star next to the name of the continent the United States is located on.

A Map of the World

Before Columbus sailed across the Atlantic Ocean, Europeans knew about only three continents—Europe, Africa, and Asia. **Continents** are Earth's largest land areas. Over time, people have learned that there are seven continents. The seven continents are Africa, Antarctica, Asia, Australia, Europe, North America, and South America.

Canada

4

ATLANTIC OCEAN

PACIFIC OCEAN

NORTH AMERICA

United States

2

1

3 Bahamas

SOUTH AMERICA

You can see the general shapes and positions of the continents and oceans on a world map. This map highlights places you have learned about.

1 St. Augustine is a city in northern Florida.
2 Jamestown is a city in Virginia.
3 San Salvador is an island in the Bahamas.
4 Québec is a city in Canada.
5 England is part of the United Kingdom. It is on an island that is part of Europe.
6 Rome is a city in Italy. It is on the continent of Europe.

Knowing the continents will help you find places on a map of the world. For example, European explorers traveled from England, France, and Spain. They explored different regions in North America. **Regions** are places that have common characteristics.

Most of Earth is covered by water. Most of this water is in the oceans. Earth's five oceans are the Arctic, Atlantic, Indian, Pacific, and Southern Oceans.

TextWork

❹ On the map, draw a box around the locations of Spain, England, and France.

❺ On the map, draw an X near the four places in North America that you learned explorers visited in Unit 4.

❻ On the map, underline the names of each of the five oceans.

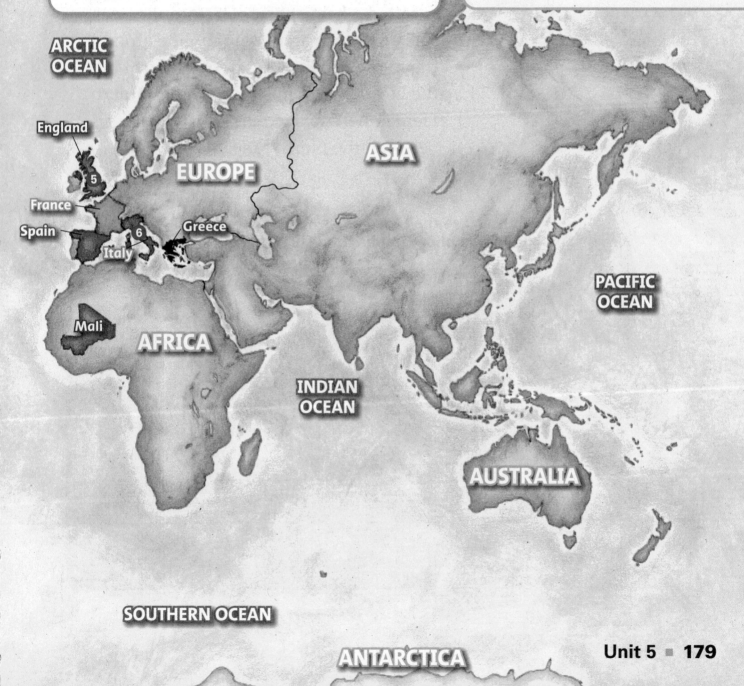

ARCTIC OCEAN

England

EUROPE

ASIA

5

France

Spain

6

Italy

Greece

Mali

AFRICA

PACIFIC OCEAN

INDIAN OCEAN

AUSTRALIA

SOUTHERN OCEAN

ANTARCTICA

The Four Hemispheres

In photographs taken from space, we can see that Earth is shaped like a sphere, or ball. Like Earth, a globe has the shape of a sphere. A globe is a model of Earth. It shows the true shapes of the oceans and continents.

The Northern and Southern Hemispheres

On a globe, Earth can be shown divided into halves. Half of a sphere, such as Earth, is called a **hemisphere** (HEH•muh•sfeer). The **equator** is an imaginary line around the middle of Earth. It divides Earth into the Northern Hemisphere and Southern Hemisphere. The equator is halfway between the North Pole and the South Pole.

You can see the true shapes on Earth by looking at a globe (left) or in photographs from space (below).

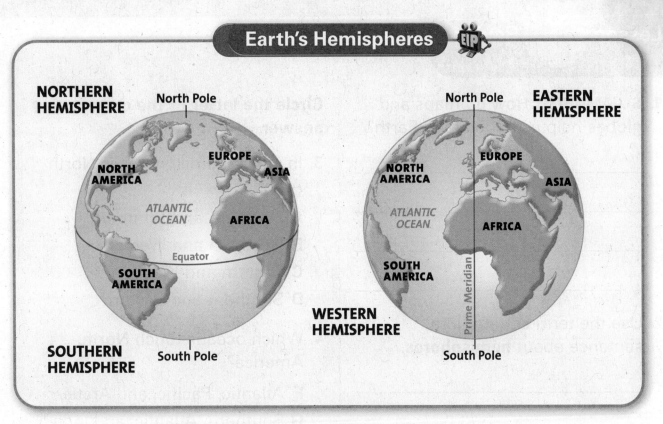

NORTHERN HEMISPHERE — North Pole

NORTH AMERICA

EUROPE

ASIA

ATLANTIC OCEAN

AFRICA

Equator

SOUTH AMERICA

SOUTHERN HEMISPHERE — South Pole

North Pole — EASTERN HEMISPHERE

NORTH AMERICA

EUROPE

ASIA

ATLANTIC OCEAN

AFRICA

SOUTH AMERICA

Prime Meridian

WESTERN HEMISPHERE

South Pole

These maps show the four hemispheres of Earth.

The Eastern and Western Hemispheres

Another way to divide Earth into hemispheres is to use the prime meridian. The **prime meridian** is an imaginary line that is often used to divide Earth into the Eastern Hemisphere and the Western Hemisphere. The prime meridian runs between the North Pole and the South Pole.

Using Hemispheres

People can use hemispheres to identify locations. The equator and the prime meridian divide Earth two different ways. They create four hemispheres. Every place on Earth is in two hemispheres. For example, North America is in the Northern Hemisphere and the Western Hemisphere.

TextWork

9 Study the map. Circle the names of the four hemispheres.

10 In which two hemispheres is North America located?

_____

_____

11 (Focus Skill) In which two hemispheres is Virginia located?

_____

_____

Unit 5 ▪ 181

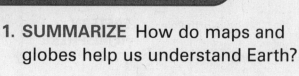

Lesson 1 Review

1. **SUMMARIZE** How do maps and globes help us understand Earth?

_____

_____

_____

_____

2. Use the term **equator** in a sentence about **hemispheres**.

_____

_____

_____

Circle the letter of the correct answer.

3. In which hemispheres is North America located?

   A Northern and Southern

   B Northern and Western

   C Eastern and Western

   D Southern and Eastern

4. Which oceans touch North America?

   F Atlantic, Pacific, and Arctic

   G Southern, Atlantic, and Indian

   H Southern, Arctic, and Indian

   J Pacific, Indian, and Arctic

Draw a line connecting each term on the left with the correct definition on the right.

5. prime meridian

6. hemisphere

7. equator

an imaginary line halfway between the North Pole and the South Pole

an imaginary line that runs between the North Pole and the South Pole

a half of Earth

An atlas of the world

activity

🖌 **Draw a World Map** Draw and color a map of the world. Label the seven continents and the five oceans.

Locating Places

Each place on Earth has a location. For example, you can use a map to show someone where you live. Maps show information geographically. **Think about how you might use maps to learn about places.**

Students locate places on a map of the world.

Essential Questions

✓ How is a simple letter-number grid system used to locate places on maps?

✓ What visual aids are used to gather, display, and classify information?

SOL **HISTORY AND SOCIAL SCIENCE SOL**
3.5e, 3.6

TextWork

❶ Draw a star near the map title on the map below.

❷ Draw a box around the map legend.

❸ Draw a circle around the compass rose. What does the compass rose show you?

_____

_____

❹ (Focus Skill) What conclusion can you draw about Lily's location?

_____

Using Maps

Maps are visual aids that show geographic information about places. Mapmakers add features to most maps. These make maps easier to understand.

Features of a Map

A map title tells the subject of the map. It may also identify the kind of map it is.

A map legend, or key, explains the map's symbols. Symbols may be colors, patterns, lines, or other special marks. They stand for real features on Earth.

A compass rose shows directions. The four main directions, or **cardinal directions**, are north, south, east, and west. A compass rose may also show **intermediate directions**. The intermediate directions are northeast, northwest, southeast, and southwest. They lie between the cardinal directions.

Name Lily
Street Jasper Lane
City Richmond
State Virginia
Country
The United States
Continent
North America

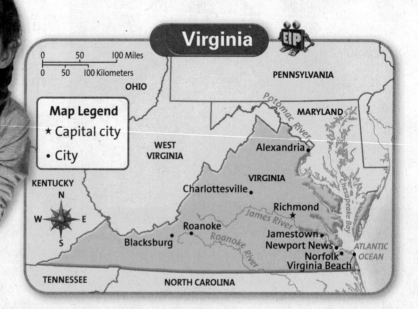

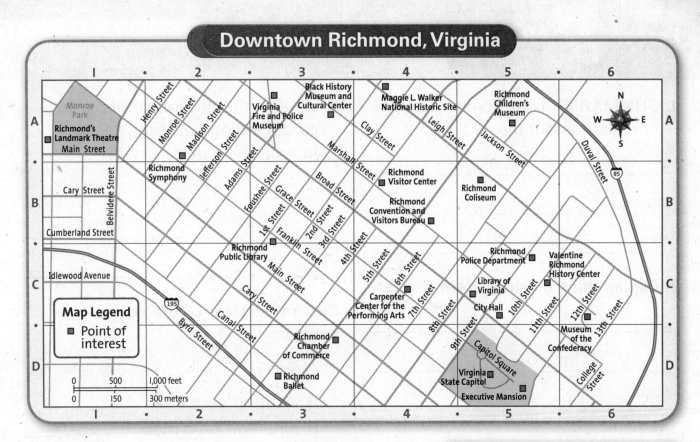

Finding Places on Maps

Geographers often put a set of lines on a map. Together, they form a grid system. A **grid system** is a set of lines the same distance apart that divides a map into small boxes. The grid system helps you find the approximate, or general, location of a place on the map.

Using a Grid System

Most map grid systems show rows and columns of boxes. Every row is labeled with a letter. Every column is labeled with a number. The approximate location of a place is given by using a letter–number pair, such as A-1 or B-3. You just trace its letter row and number column until they meet.

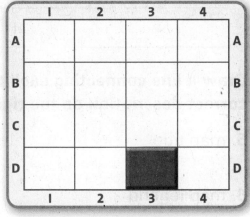

TextWork

❺ Study the grid system above. What is the location of the red box?

❻ Study the map. Circle the point of interest located at A-5.

1. SUMMARIZE How do maps help you learn about places?

_____

_____

_____

2. Explain how a **grid system** works.

_____

_____

_____

_____

_____

3. What is the difference between cardinal directions and intermediate directions?

_____

_____

_____

Circle the letter of the correct answer.

4. A grid system helps you find—

   A location on a map

   B direction on a map

   C the subject of the map

   D symbols on a map

Draw a line connecting each term on the left with the correct description on the right.

5. map title

6. map legend

7. compass rose

explains the symbols used on a map

shows directions

tells the subject of a map

A compass

activity

🖍 **Make a Map with a Grid** Draw a map of a place you know, such as your neighborhood, your school, or a room in your home. Then add a grid so that you can locate places.

Different Lands and Ways of Life

You have learned about the lands of ancient Greece, Rome, and the empire of Mali. You have learned about the places in North America where Europeans explored. Every environment is different. **Think about the different ways that information about environments can be shown.**

Alexandria, Virginia, along the Potomac River

Essential Questions

✓ What were the physical and human characteristics of ancient Greece and Rome and West Africa?

✓ How did the people of ancient Greece, ancient Rome, and Mali adapt to and change their environment to meet their needs?

✓ What visual aids are used to gather, display, and classify information?

✓ How do producers use natural, human, and capital resources to produce goods and services?

SOL **HISTORY AND SOCIAL SCIENCE SOL**
3.4b, 3.4c, 3.6, 3.7

Each Place Is Special

All places on Earth have characteristics that make them special. You can describe any place by telling about them.

Characteristics of a Place

Virginia, like other places, has different kinds of physical characteristics. These include land and water. Most places also have different human characteristics. Some of these are roads, bridges, buildings, farms, and cities.

Pictures Show Geographic Information

Maps are one way to show geographic information. Pictures are another kind of visual aid that you can use to gather and display geographic information. Pictures help you see how places look.

TextWork

❶ Underline the two kinds of characteristics that describe a place.

❷ Study the map. What physical characteristics are near where you live?

_____

_____

Virginia's Land

You can use maps and pictures to learn what a place looks like. Virginia has valleys, mountains, and beaches.

Valleys

Mountains

ALLEGHENY MOUNTAINS

APPALACHIAN MOUNTAINS

Blue Ridge Mountains

Monterey

Grundy

Blacksburg

Roanoke

Big Stone Gap

Wytheville

Abingdon

Bristol

Martinsville

N W E S

0   20   40 Miles
0   20   40 Kilometers

Graphs Show Geographic Information

You can also use graphs to show how places are similar and different. Some geographic information is easier to understand if it is shown in a graph.

A bar graph uses bars to show numbers or amounts of things. Each bar stands for a different thing. You read some bar graphs from bottom to top.

A circle graph, or pie graph, is shaped like a circle. It looks like a sliced pie. Each slice shows a part of the whole. You can easily see how the parts relate to one another and to the whole subject.

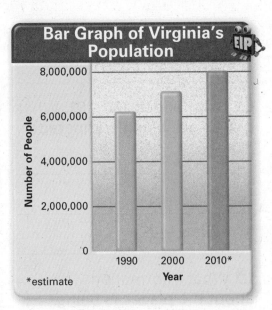

Bar Graph of Virginia's Population

Number of People — 8,000,000, 6,000,000, 4,000,000, 2,000,000, 0

Year — 1990, 2000, 2010*

*estimate

Circle Graph of Virginia's Population

People living in cities

People living in the countryside

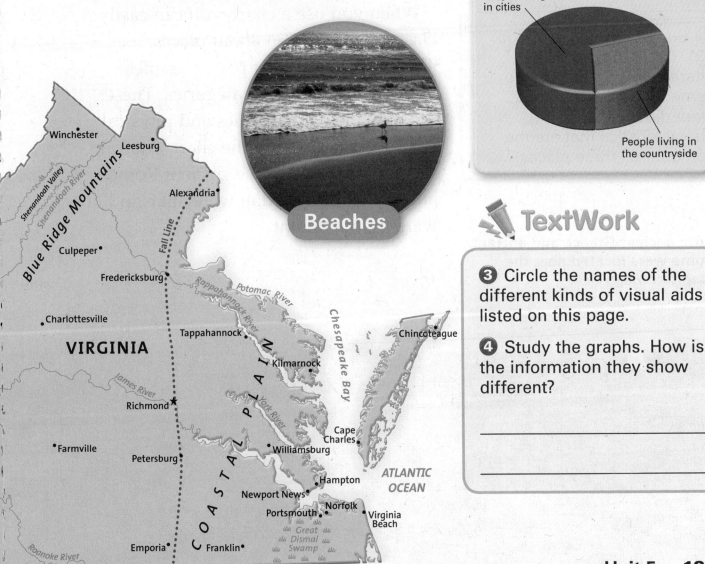

Beaches

Winchester
Leesburg
Shenandoah Valley
Shenandoah River
Blue Ridge Mountains
Alexandria
Fall Line
Culpeper
Fredericksburg
Rappahannock River
Potomac River
Charlottesville
Tappahannock
Chincoteague
VIRGINIA
Kilmarnock
Chesapeake Bay
James River
C O A S T A L   P L A I N
York River
Richmond
Cape Charles
Farmville
Williamsburg
Petersburg
ATLANTIC OCEAN
Hampton
Newport News
Portsmouth
Norfolk
Virginia Beach
Roanoke River
Emporia
Franklin
Great Dismal Swamp

TextWork

3 Circle the names of the different kinds of visual aids listed on this page.

4 Study the graphs. How is the information they show different?

_____

_____

Places Affect People

People in different places develop different ways of life. The physical and human characteristics of any location affect the way people live there.

Charts Show Geographic Information

You have used visual aids such as maps, pictures, and graphs to learn about places. Charts are another kind of visual aid. They show information in an organized way. A chart can help you understand a lot of information quickly. Sometimes tables and graphs are called charts.

When you use a chart, you can easily classify information about places. The chart on the next page classifies information into two categories. These are human characteristics and physical characteristics. Using the chart, you can see how ancient Greece, ancient Rome, and the empire of Mali were alike and how were they different.

5 Skim pages 190–191. What places are being compared?

_____

_____

_____

6 What information about the places is being compared?

_____

_____

7 Study the chart on page 191. Circle the physical characteristics that are the same for all three places. Underline the human characteristics that are the same for all three places.

Both ancient Greece and ancient Rome were located near the Mediterranean Sea.

Comparing Ancient Places

Place	Physical Characteristics	Human Characteristics
Ancient Greece In southern Europe	• Near Mediterranean Sea • On a peninsula • Many islands • Mountains and hills • Limited rich soil	• City-states • Farmers • Shipbuilders • Traders • Fishers • Potters
Ancient Rome In southern Europe	• Near Mediterranean Sea • On a peninsula • Next to river • Built on many hills • Limited rich soil	• Cities • Farmers • Road builders • Traders • Fishers • Potters
Empire of Mali In West Africa	• Spread from desert to savanna • Near rivers • Gold • Salt • Limited rich soil	• Cities • Farmers • Miners • Traders

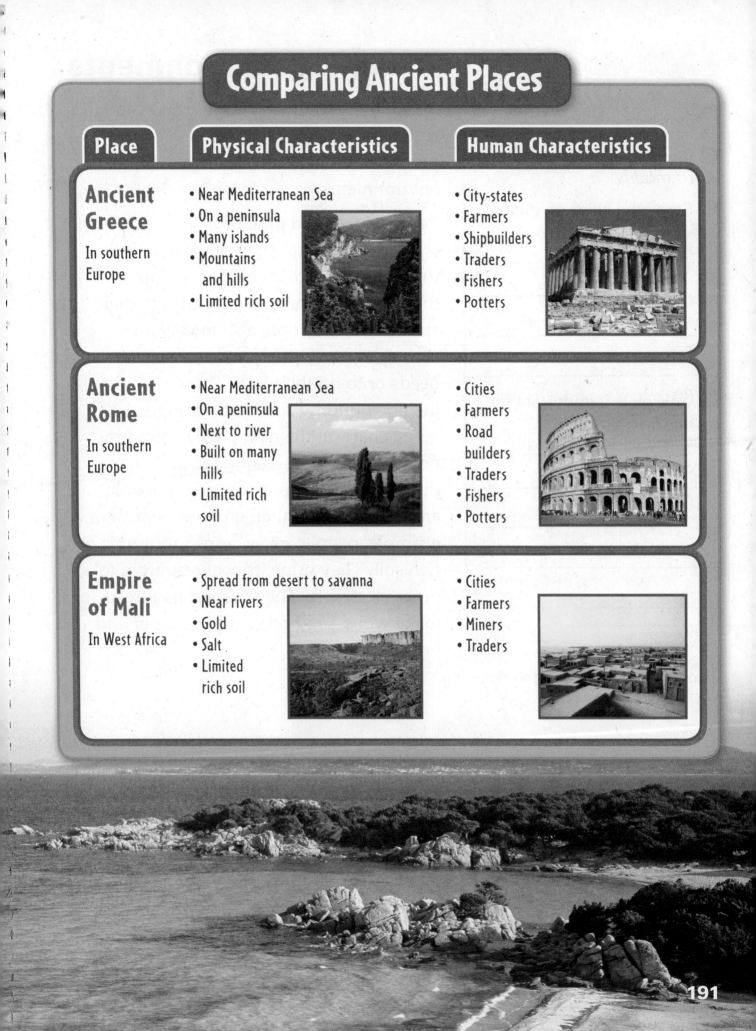

8 Circle the definition of the word *modify*.

9 Study the chart on page 193. What are some ways people modify land?

_____

_____

_____

10 Focus Skill Why is it important for people to adapt to and modify their environment?

_____

_____

_____

_____

Jamestown was built along the James River.

Changing Environments

People use natural, human, and capital resources to meet their needs. However, people often make changes to their environments to use those resources.

People Adapt and Modify

All people adapt their ways of living to fit their environment. They adapt their foods, clothing, and homes to their environment. People also **modify**, or change, the environment to meet their needs or to do their jobs. These changes include building roads and bridges.

The chart on the next page shows how people of the past adapted to and changed their environments. Even today, people are still changing their environments. For example, people grow crops in Virginia's rich soil. They mine its coal resources to make electricity. They harvest its forests to make wood products, such as paper and lumber.

Comparing Environments of Places

Environment	Adapt	Modify
Ancient Greece Islands, mountains, hills, sea, mild climate	Settled between mountains, and traded on the sea	Built terraces
Ancient Rome Hills, rivers, sea, mild climate	Built city on hills, and traded on the sea	Built roads, bridges, and aqueducts
Empire of Mali Savanna, desert, rivers, mostly dry climate	Traded across the savanna and desert 	Dug mines for gold and salt 
Jamestown Settlement Wetland, rivers, near ocean, moderate climate	Traded on rivers and on the ocean 	Cut trees, and built a fort, houses, and roads 

1. **SUMMARIZE** What are different ways to show information about the environment?

_____

_____

_____

2. Explain the difference between adapt and **modify**.

_____

_____

_____

3. How did people in ancient times modify the land?

_____

_____

_____

4. Why is it important to protect the environment?

_____

_____

_____

Draw a line connecting each term on the left with the correct description on the right.

5. bar graph   uses parts of a circle to show information

6. chart   uses bars to show the numbers or amounts of things

7. circle graph   shows information in a table or other organized way

writing

Make Visual Aids Make a chart showing the number of boys and the number of girls in your class. Then use the information to make a bar graph and a circle graph. Explain your graphs.

Welcome to Virginia

Specialization and Trade

People make goods and provide services by using the resources that are available. People cannot make everything they need and want. They must trade to get the things they do not have. **Think about why people trade with one another.**

Apples are grown on this orchard in Virginia.

Essential Questions

✓ How do producers use natural, human, and capital resources to produce goods and services?

✓ What is specialization?

✓ Why do those who specialize have to depend on others?

✓ Why do people trade?

SOL **HISTORY AND SOCIAL SCIENCE SOL**
3.7, 3.8

TextWork

❶ Underline the sentence that tells what an economy is.

❷ Circle the sentence that has examples of service jobs.

❸ (Focus Skill) Use information from the circle graph to draw a conclusion about Virginia's workers.

_____

_____

_____

A police officer is a service worker.

Learning About the Economy

The way a community, state, or country makes and uses goods and services is called its **economy**. Resources are an important part of the economy.

Using Resources

Producers use three kinds of resources to produce goods and services. They use natural, human, and capital resources.

More than 6,000 businesses in Virginia make goods. Examples of Virginia goods include computers and electronic products, boats, trucks, baked goods, and paper. Most goods are made in factories.

Today, most people in Virginia work in service jobs. Teachers, doctors, and police officers are examples of people who provide services.

Virginia's Workers, 2008

Workers who provide services

Workers who make goods

Children in History

Child Workers in Virginia

In the early 1900s, many children worked in mines and factories. Some children worked long hours using unsafe machines. Because the children were working, they did not go to school. Photographer Lewis Hine took pictures of children working in Virginia and in other states. When people saw these pictures, they wanted to change things. In the 1930s and 1940s, laws were passed to protect children and help keep them in school.

Make It Relevant **Why do you think it is important for children to go to school instead of work?**

People Work Together

Think about how busy you would be if you had to make all the things you use every day. In ancient times, people had to make most of what they used themselves. Later, as towns grew, they were able to share the work with others in their communities.

People in Virginia communities depend on producers to make goods and provide services. A person who buys a good or service is a **consumer**.

Producers and consumers in a community depend on one another. Producers depend on consumers to buy the goods, or products, they make. Consumers depend on producers to provide goods and services for them to buy.

TextWork

❹ How are you a consumer?

_____

_____

❺ What is the difference between a producer and a consumer?

_____

_____

_____

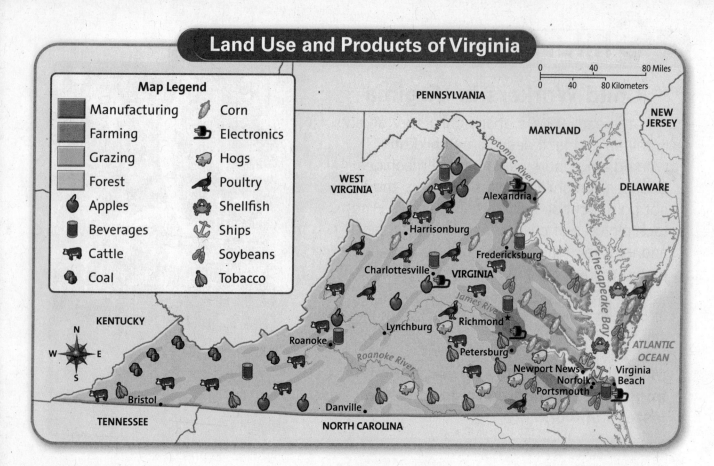

Land Use and Products of Virginia

Map Legend

Manufacturing	Corn
Farming	Electronics
Grazing	Hogs
Forest	Poultry
Apples	Shellfish
Beverages	Ships
Cattle	Soybeans
Coal	Tobacco

TextWork

6 Find the term *land use* and explain what it means using your own words.

_____

_____

_____

7 Study the map. How is most of the land around Roanoke used?

_____

_____

Places Affect People

People living in a region cannot make all the things they need. This is because resources are spread unevenly across Earth. In any region, people use the most plentiful resources. Businesses decide what product to make or what service to provide based on the resources available.

To find out where resources are located and how they are used, geographers look at land use. **Land use** is the way most of the land in a region is used.

A land use and products map can help you learn about the economy of a region. The map legend uses colors to show different land use. It also uses symbols to show where products are grown or made.

Different Regions, Different Resources

All three kinds of resources affect the producers of goods and services in any place. Some regions have many natural resources. Others have many skilled workers, or human resources. Most businesses need buildings, machines, tools, and other capital resources.

The region where you live has its own natural, human, and capital resources. Western Virginia has thick forests, scenic drives, coal resources, and cattle farms. Eastern Virginia has waterways, beaches, and a large population. Northern Virginia is a center for education, high-tech, and government jobs. Central and southern Virginia both have historic towns and rich farmland.

TextWork

8 Use the map on page 198. Find the area on the map that includes your community. Circle the area.

9 How is most of the land in your region used?

_____

10 What are some products grown or made in or near your region?

_____

_____

Scientists at NASA's Langley Research Center in Hampton, Virginia, work to meet challenges in space and on Earth.

Goods from Virginia are shipped to other parts of the world from this port in Newport News.

What's So Special?

Sometimes a community becomes well known because of a successful product. Focusing on producing one kind of good or service is called **specialization**.

Specialization Works

Specialization encourages trade between people and regions. People making mostly one kind of product or providing one kind of service must depend on others. They must trade with others to get goods or services they do not produce themselves.

People often specialize in making things they can trade. People trade when individuals and groups will benefit from that trade. To **benefit** is to get something good. People trade to get things they need and want but do not have.

TextWork

11 Underline the definition of the word *specialization*.

12 (Focus Skill) Draw a conclusion about how specialization encourages trade.

_____

_____

_____

Virginia Specializes

Specialization allows people and regions to make the best use of available resources. By trading, they also get the most out of **scarce**, or hard-to-find, resources. These include resources such as coal and oil.

Different regions specialize in different goods and services. For example, many people in eastern Virginia work in tourism. This region specializes in services for visitors to the historic sites, parks, and beaches. The area around Charlottesville specializes in education and research. Much of southern Virginia specializes in agriculture. Food products such as Virginia peanuts are grown there and sold around the world.

TextWork

13 Use the word *scarce* in a sentence about natural resources.

_____

_____

_____

14 (Focus Skill) Why do you think regions specialize in different goods and services?

_____

_____

_____

_____

Biography

Responsibility

Dr. Robin Felder EIP

Dr. Robin Felder lives in Charlottesville, Virginia. His father taught him how to make things out of pewter, a kind of metal. Today, he is a doctor, a teacher, and a high-tech inventor. He works at the University of Virginia Medical Center. Dr. Felder has improved health care by specializing in inventing robots that help people.

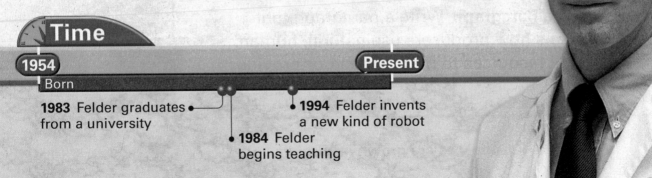

Time

1954 — Present
Born

1983 Felder graduates from a university

1984 Felder begins teaching

1994 Felder invents a new kind of robot

1. **SUMMARIZE** Why do people trade?

_____

_____

_____

2. Write a sentence using the word **specialization**.

_____

_____

_____

Circle the letter of the correct answer.

3. Which of these is a capital resource?

    A Trucks

    B Workers

    C Peanuts

    D Coal

4. Which of these is a human resource?

    F Forests

    G Coal mines

    H High-tech workers

    J Buildings

Draw a line connecting each kind of resource on the left with the correct examples of the resource on the right.

5. natural resources   factories and offices

6. human resources   teachers and doctors

7. capital resources   rivers and bays

writing

Write a Paragraph Write a paragraph that explains how producers use natural, human, and capital resources to make a good or provide a service.

Raspberries are grown in Virginia.

Making Economic Choices

People must make choices about how they earn, spend, and save money. Families make economic decisions every day. **Think about how you earn, spend, and save money.**

These children use money to buy bread in a bakery.

Essential Question
✓ Why does an economic choice involve giving up something else?

 HISTORY AND SOCIAL SCIENCE SOL
3.9

TextWork

1 (Focus Skill) Draw a conclusion about why people must make economic choices.

_____

_____

_____

2 Use your own words to explain the term *income*.

_____

_____

_____

3 Study the bar graph. Circle the type of job in Virginia that has the most workers.

Earn, Spend, and Save

People must make economic choices because they cannot have everything they want. An **economic choice** is a decision about earning, spending, or saving money. When you make an economic choice, you choose from among different possibilities to decide what you want.

People work to earn money they can use to buy goods and services. The money they are paid for their work is called **income**.

People use their income to buy the things they use every day. A person must spend much of his or her income on food, clothes, and housing. Then he or she can choose how to use the money that is left.

People may decide to save part of their income. Saving is important because things can happen that are not expected.

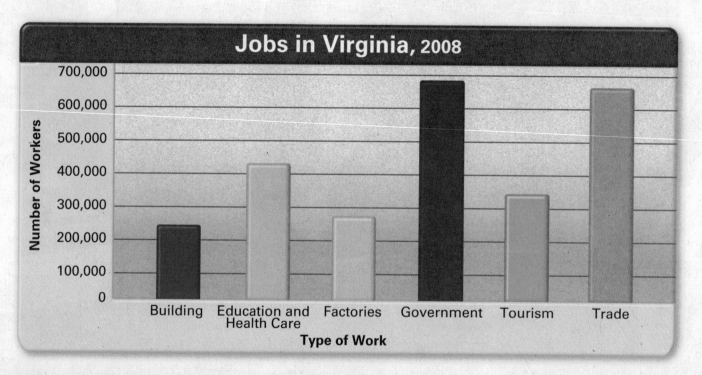

Jobs in Virginia, 2008

Earn

The parents in this family work to earn a living. The mother owns a photography business.

Spend

The members of this family use part of their income to buy things they need, such as food.

Save

This family puts some of the money it saves into a bank.

Opportunity Cost

4 What is an opportunity cost?

_____

_____

_____

All economic choices require giving up something else. When you choose to buy or do one thing, you give up the chance to buy or do something else. The next best choice that is given up when a decision is made is called the **opportunity cost**.

Making Wise Choices

You can learn to make wise economic choices. There are some things you should think about before making an economic choice. You should compare the costs and advantages of each choice.

It is important to think about the costs and benefits before making an economic choice.

Making Economic Choices

Choices	Choice Made	Opportunity Cost
Ice cream or popcorn	Ice cream	Popcorn
Toy or favorite video	Favorite video	Toy
Spend money now or save for the future	Spend now	Save for the future

Economic choices have two kinds of costs. One is the money you will pay for a product or a service. The other is the opportunity cost, or the choice that is given up. You should also think about the benefits of, or what you will gain from, each choice.

Think About It

When you buy something at a store, you are making an economic choice. You choose which thing you will spend your money on. At the same time, your opportunity cost is the thing you will not spend that money on.

Each time you spend money, think about what you are giving up. Knowing how to make good economic choices can help you spend and save wisely.

Plan Ahead

Having a plan can help you make good economic choices. A plan for spending and saving money is called a **budget**. A budget can help you decide the best way to use your money.

TextWork

5 Give an example of what you gave up when you bought a product or a service. Why did you give up what you did?

_____

_____

_____

6 Study the table. Circle what the opportunity cost is of spending money now.

7 Underline the sentence that tells what a budget is.

Make a Budget

People of all ages can make and use a simple budget. First, get a notebook in which to record your information. This will help you keep track of your money.

Next, make a two-column chart in your notebook. Label the top of the first column "Incoming Money." Write down all of your income. For example, money you earned by working and money that was a gift.

Write "Outgoing Money" at the top of the second column. List all the ways you spend money. Each time you spend money, record it in your budget.

Finally, total the amounts in each column. Your incoming total is how much you have, which you can spend or save. Your outgoing total is what you spent. The money you have left is your savings.

❽ Put the steps for making a budget in the correct order.

_____ Make a two-column chart in your notebook.

_____ List all the ways you spend money.

_____ Write down all your income.

_____ Total the amounts in both columns.

_____ Get a notebook to record your information.

This family works together to make a budget.

Economic Goals

You can use a budget to see how you are spending money. You can also use it to help you reach an economic goal, such as buying a new bicycle. Think about the things you would like to buy or do in the future.

Record these economic goals on a special page in your budget notebook. Keeping your goals in mind is the best way to make wise economic decisions.

This boy saves money to reach his economic goals.

Lesson 5 Review

1. **SUMMARIZE** Why do people make economic choices?

   _____

   _____

2. How does **income** affect a **budget**?

   _____

   _____

3. Why does an economic choice involve giving something up?

   _____

   _____

4. Describe an economic decision you have made.

   _____

   _____

activity

Make a Budget Make a sample budget to reach an economic goal. Set a goal to buy or do something special. Then follow the steps in the lesson to create a plan for reaching that goal.

Fun with Social Studies

Map Facts

Use the grid to find the missing letters of the Map Facts. Then, use the letters in yellow to find a nickname of the continent.

Map Facts Grid

	1	2	3	4	5
A	a	b	c	d	e
B	f	g	h	i	j
C	k	l	m	n	o
D	p	q	r	s	t
E	u	v	w	x	y

What is the coldest continent?

☐ ☐ ☐ ☐ ☐ ☐ ☐ ☐ ☐ ☐
A-1 C-4 D-5 A-1 D-3 A-3 D-5 B-4 A-3 A-1

Which ocean surrounds the continent above?

☐ ☐ ☐ ☐ ☐ ☐ ☐ **Ocean**
D-4 C-5 E-1 D-5 B-3 A-5 D-3 C-4

L ☐☐ D ☐ F P ☐☐ G ☐☐ N S

Connect the Dots

Trace the directions below to find out what is in the water.

1. Go southeast 2 dots.
2. Go east 3 dots.
3. Go northeast 2 dots.
4. Go west 3 dots.
5. Go north 5 dots.
6. Go southwest 4 dots.
7. Go east 4 dots.
8. Go south 1 dot.
9. Go west 4 dots.

START

N NW NE W E SW SE S

Go-Together Tic-Tac-Toe

Which three terms go together? Draw a line to make a tic-tac-toe.

Tic-Tac-Toe

economy	income	prime meridian
resources	hemisphere	consumer
equator	economic choice	goods and services

Woof Wash

Each player starts a service that specializes in dog-washing. Take turns using a spinner. Each player adds or subtracts points from his or her total score.

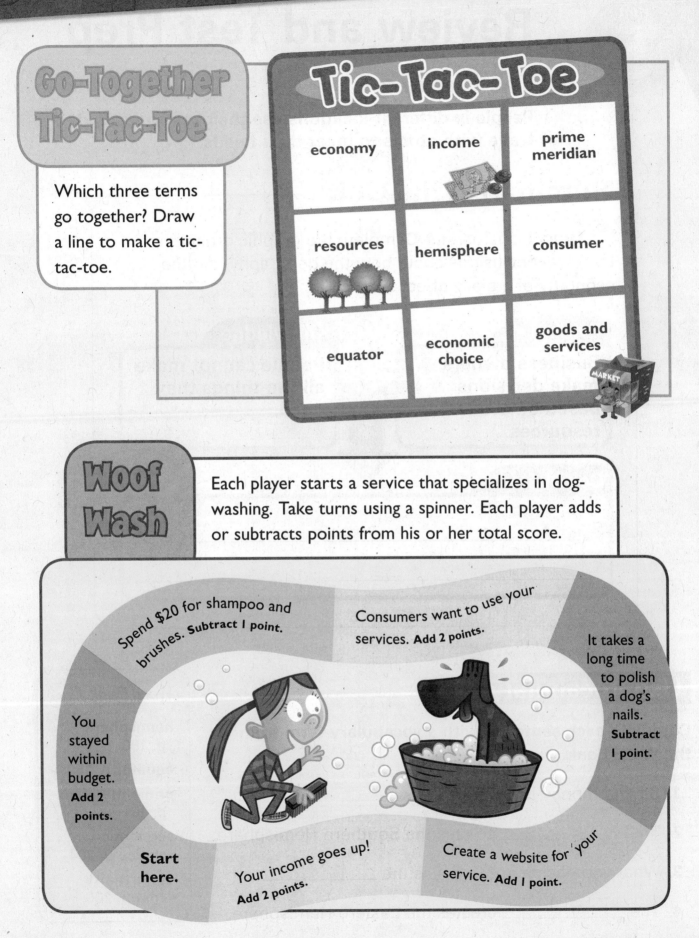

Spend $20 for shampoo and brushes. **Subtract 1 point.**

Consumers want to use your services. **Add 2 points.**

It takes a long time to polish a dog's nails. **Subtract 1 point.**

You stayed within budget. **Add 2 points.**

Start here.

Your income goes up! **Add 2 points.**

Create a website for your service. **Add 1 point.**

Review and Test Prep

The Big Idea

People in different locations use their resources and trade with others to meet their needs.

Summarize the Unit

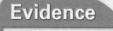 **Draw Conclusions** Complete the graphic organizer to draw conclusions about how the geography and the economy of a place affect each other.

Evidence

Business owners make decisions based on available resources.

Knowledge

People cannot make all the things they need.

Conclusion

_____

_____

Use Vocabulary

Complete each sentence with a vocabulary term from the Word Bank.

1. Saving money is a wise _____.

2. The _____ creates the Southern Hemisphere.

3. What you decide not to buy is the _____.

4. The _____ creates the Eastern Hemisphere.

Word Bank

hemisphere p. 180

equator p. 180

prime meridian p. 181

economic choice p. 204

opportunity cost p. 206

Think About It

Circle the letter of the correct answer.

5.
- **England**
- **France**
- **Spain**

These countries are in—

A Europe

B North America

C Africa

D Asia

6. The empire of Mali was in—

F North America

G Asia

H Africa

J Europe

7.

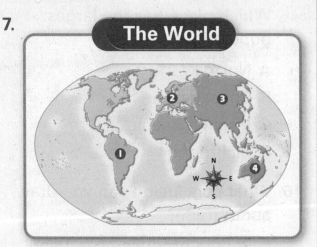

The World

Which number on this map shows where Asia is located?

A 1

B 2

C 3

D 4

8.

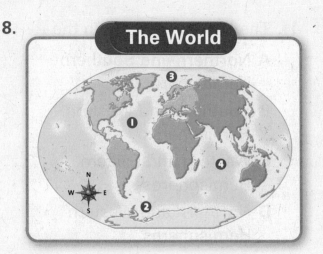

The World

Which number on this map shows where the Southern Ocean is located?

F 1

G 2

H 3

J 4

9. Which oceans border the United States?

A Atlantic, Indian, and Pacific

B Arctic, Atlantic, and Pacific

C Arctic, Indian, and Pacific

D Atlantic, Pacific, and Southern

10. What is half of Earth called?

F Prime meridian

G Continent

H Equator

J Hemisphere

11. The United States is in the—

A Northern and Southern Hemispheres

B Southern and Western Hemispheres

C Western and Eastern Hemispheres

D Northern and Western Hemispheres

12. Intermediate directions on a map can be found by looking at a—

F scale

G title

H compass rose

J legend

13.

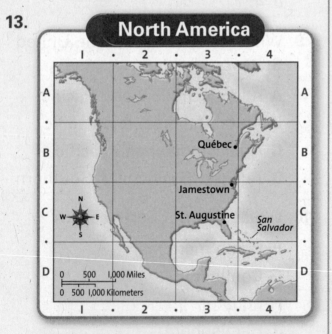

Which of the following places is located at B-3?

A San Salvador

B St. Augustine

C Québec

D Jamestown

14. On a map, a grid system is used to—

F help users locate places

G help users know symbols

H show directions

J show distances

15.

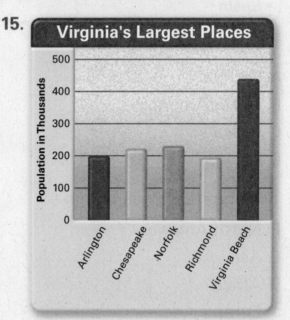

Which place has the largest population?

A Norfolk

B Chesapeake

C Virginia Beach

D Richmond

16. What conclusion can you draw about trade?

F People produce everything they need.

G People trade for the things they cannot produce.

H People do not usually benefit from trade.

J People try hard not to specialize.

17. Specialization is—

A working together to get things done

B trading one kind of product for another

C producing one kind of good or service

D giving up one choice to get another

18. What is the MAIN reason people trade?

F To get things they do not have

G To get things they already have

H To help others

J To learn about others

19. An economic choice is a decision about—

A earning, spending, or saving

B only earning

C only spending

D only earning and spending

20.

Sara wanted to buy a skateboard. She also wanted to buy a book by her favorite author. She decided to buy the skateboard.

In this paragraph, the opportunity cost is the—

F book

G money

H author

J skateboard

Answer these questions.

21. How do maps and globes help you understand more about the places you have studied?

_____

_____

22. How does specialization lead to trade?

_____

_____

23. What economic choice have you made? What was the opportunity cost?

_____

_____

Watch out for that alligator. Look at those teeth!

Help Eco win a race across the United States. In this game, you'll need to use the map and globe skills you've learned in the unit. Can you keep Eco moving in the right direction and avoid roadside dangers? Go online to play the game now.

Show What You Know

✏ Writing Write a Newspaper Article

Write a newspaper article about economic specialization in your community. Tell how specialization works. Then find out about what goods and services your community specializes in. Use what you find out to write your article.

🖌 Activity Make an Atlas

Make an atlas using what you have learned in this unit. First, create a world map that shows the seven continents and the five oceans. Next, create a second world map that shows the equator, the prime meridian, and the four hemispheres. Then, create a third world map that shows the countries the European explorers sailed from and the areas they explored. Make sure all of your maps have titles, legends, and compass roses. Add to your atlas at least one other visual aid, such as a grid map, table, graph, chart, or picture.

Citizens and Government

People celebrate
the Fourth of July in
Washington, D.C.

Spotlight on Standards

THE BIG IDEA The American people are
united by common beliefs and experiences.

HISTORY AND SOCIAL SCIENCE SOL
3.10a, 3.10b, 3.10c, 3.11a, 3.11b, 3.11c, 3.11d, 3.12

Set the Stage

1 Circle the name of the person who was the first African American Supreme Court justice.

2 Underline the name of the person who founded a group that helped farm workers.

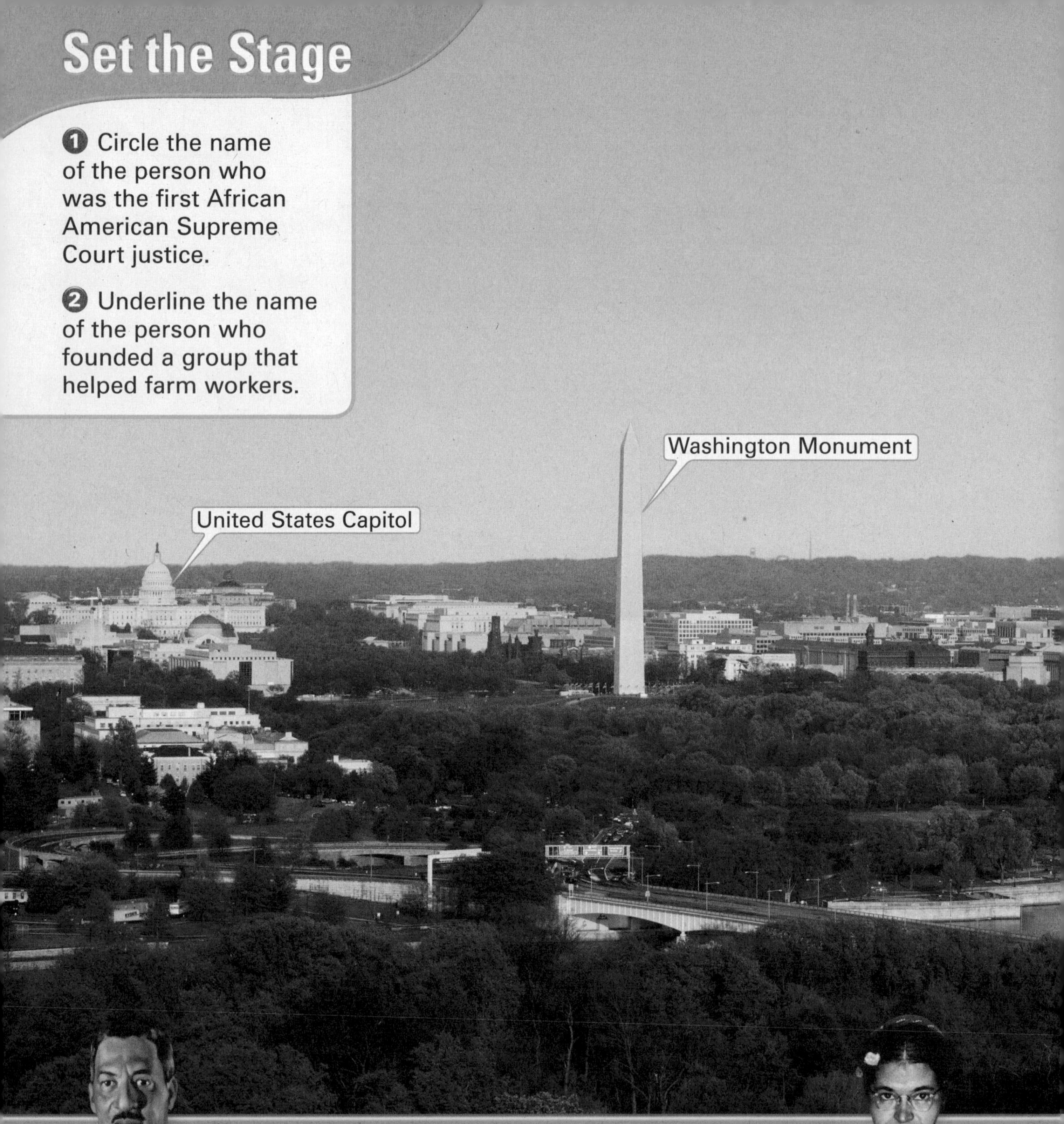

Washington Monument

United States Capitol

Thurgood Marshall
The first African American justice of the United States Supreme Court

Rosa Parks
Community leader who helped African Americans gain rights

Washington, D.C., is our nation's capital.

Jefferson Memorial

Lincoln Memorial

Dr. Martin Luther King, Jr.
Leader who led peaceful marches for people's rights

César Chávez
Founder of a group that improved the lives of many farm workers

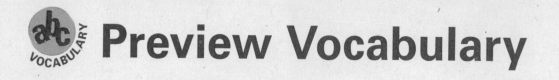

Preview Vocabulary

community

A **community** is a place where people live, work, and play. p. 223

rules and laws

Rules tell people what they must or must not do. Important rules are called **laws**. p. 224

government

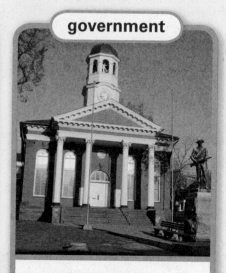

A **government** makes, carries out, and decides if rules and laws have been broken. p. 224

citizen

Citizens are the people who live in a community, a state, or a nation. p. 225

republican form of government

A **republican form of government** is a representative democracy. p. 231

diverse

Citizens of the United States are **diverse**. They are different from one another. p. 260

Reading Social Studies

Generalize

Learn

When you **generalize**, you make a general statement about a group of ideas. To generalize, you first look at all the facts. Then you decide what the facts all tell about.

Facts

Fact	Fact	Fact

Generalization

General statement about the facts

Practice

Write a generalization for each paragraph. The first paragraph has been done for you.

Many Virginians choose to work without pay. They help improve their communities. — **Facts**

Generalize: Many Virginians work without pay to help their communities. — **Generalize**

Some people help at schools and hospitals. Others help clean up parks. There is always a lot to be done.

Generalize: _____

Apply

Read the following paragraphs. Then complete the activities below.

Virginia Corps

People often want to donate, or give, their time and skills to a good cause. Many Virginians who want to help improve their state join Virginia Corps. A *corps* (KOHR) is a group of people working together to reach a goal.

State leaders formed Virginia Corps in 2002. Virginia Corps connects people to projects that help Virginia.

Members of Virginia Corps can take part in different ways. Many choose to work on preparing for emergencies. These members learn how to fight fires, give first aid, and rescue people. Other members help make communities safer. They might become a school crossing guard. Many doctors and nurses donate their skills, too. They help out in difficult times, such as after a hurricane.

Former Governor Tim Kaine supports Virginia Corps. He has said about its members, "Virginia relies on these volunteers and their excellent projects."

1. **From the first paragraph, what generalization can you make about people and Virginia Corps?**

_____

_____

_____

_____

2. **Underline the sentence that supports the generalization that Virginia Corps is important to Virginia.**

Why Government Is Important

Most people live in communities. A **community** is a place where people live, work, and play. Communities need many things to run smoothly. **Think about the things that make communities better places to live.**

A community in Fairfax County, Virginia

Essential Questions

✓ What is government?
✓ What are the basic purposes of government?
✓ Why is government necessary?
✓ What are some basic principles commonly held by American citizens?

HISTORY AND SOCIAL SCIENCE SOL
3.10a, 3.10b, 3.10c, 3.11a, 3.11c

Rules and Laws

Schools, businesses, clubs, and families often make rules. **Rules** tell people what they must or must not do.

Important rules are written and carried out by the government. These rules are called **laws**. A **government** is a group of people who make and carry out rules and laws. It also decides if rules and laws have been broken.

The Purposes of Rules and Laws

One purpose of rules and laws is to help keep people safe. For example, speed limits on roads help protect people.

Another purpose of rules and laws is to maintain, or keep, order. For example, laws tell drivers which side of the road to travel on. At school, raising your hand before speaking in class is a rule.

❶ Use the word *rule* in a sentence about a rule at your school or home.

_____

_____

_____

❷ (Focus Skill) How are rules and laws related?

_____

_____

_____

❸ Circle two purposes of rules and laws.

Levels of Government

Local

Richmond

Government

A government serves its citizens. **Citizens** are the people who live in a community, a state, or a nation.

The Purpose of Government

A government has three main purposes. It makes laws, carries out laws, and decides if laws have been broken. Governments are necessary because they protect the rights and property of citizens. A **right** is a freedom.

In the United States, there are three levels of government—local, state, and national. A local government serves a community. Each of the 50 states, including Virginia, has a state government. The national government serves all of the United States. Each level of government makes laws for the citizens it serves.

TextWork

❹ Underline the text that explains the meaning of the word *right*.

❺ Scan this page. Circle the names of the three main levels of government. How are they alike? How are they different?

_____

_____

_____

❻ Study the diagram. Which level of government serves the city of Richmond?

_____

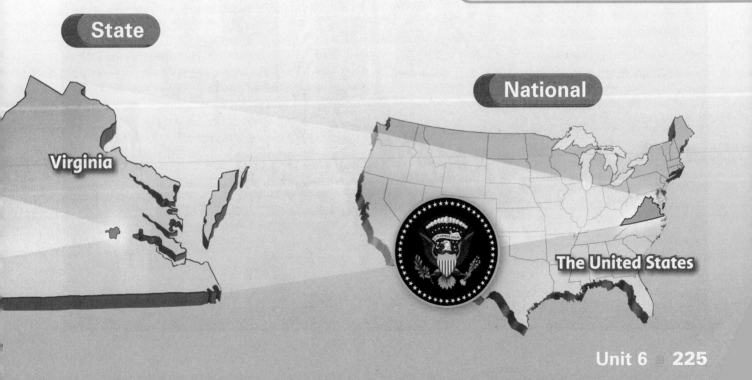

State

Virginia

National

The United States

People Have Rights

Every citizen of the United States has certain rights. A citizen is born with these rights. They may not be taken away.

Basic Principles

Early leaders of the United States listed some basic principles held by American citizens. A **principle** is an idea that people believe in. All citizens of the United States have the right to "Life, Liberty, and the pursuit of Happiness." *Liberty* means "freedom." *Pursuit* is the action of working towards something.

Another basic principle held by citizens of the United States is **equality under the law**. This means that all people are to be treated fairly.

7 Underline the text that explains the meaning of the word *principle*.

8 Why is the basic principle of *equality under the law* important?

_____

_____

_____

_____

People view the Constitution and other early documents.

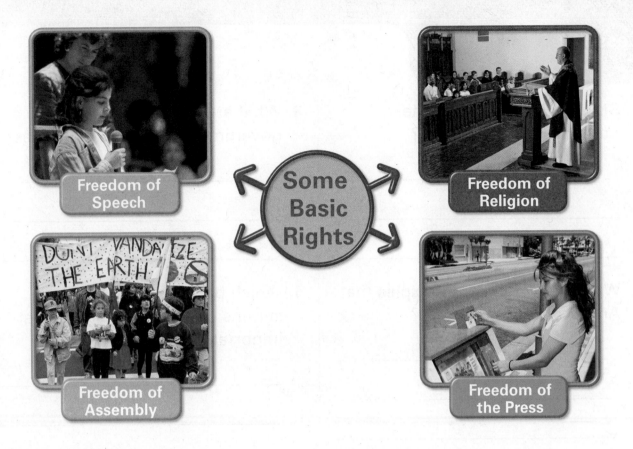

Some Basic Rights

Freedom of Speech

Freedom of Religion

Freedom of Assembly

Freedom of the Press

DON'T VANDALIZE THE EARTH

The Bill of Rights

In 1787, our nation's first leaders wrote the Constitution of the United States. A **constitution** is a set of laws that tell how a government will work. To protect the rights of citizens, the leaders added the Bill of Rights to the Constitution.

The Bill of Rights lists many freedoms that United States citizens have. Freedom of speech allows citizens to speak freely about their ideas. Freedom of the press allows people to write, read, and watch what they want. Freedom of assembly allows people to assemble, or meet, peacefully in a group. Freedom of religion means that all citizens are free to follow any religion or no religion. Americans have other basic rights as well.

TextWork

9 Why did our nation's first leaders add the Bill of Rights to the Constitution?

_____

_____

_____

_____

10 Study the diagram. Circle the right that allows people to meet peacefully in a group.

1. **SUMMARIZE** What are the purposes of government?

   _____

   _____

   _____

2. What are two basic **principles** that American citizens live by?

   _____

   _____

   _____

3. What are the three levels of government in the United States?

   _____

   _____

   _____

4. Which basic right of American citizens do you think is the most important? Tell why.

   _____

   _____

   _____

Draw a line connecting each freedom on the left with the correct example of the freedom on the right.

5. freedom of speech   to believe anything you want

6. freedom of the press   to read and watch what you want

7. freedom of religion   to say in public what you believe

activity

Make a Word Web Make a word web of the ideas that people in the United States believe in. Include some basic principles and rights.

The city seal of Harrisonburg

Three American Presidents

Over time, many Americans have worked to defend our basic principles. Three leaders who made important contributions are George Washington, Thomas Jefferson, and Abraham Lincoln. **Think about how each leader worked to defend American principles.**

Mount Rushmore in South Dakota

Essential Question
✓ How did American citizens work to defend American principles?

SOL **HISTORY AND SOCIAL SCIENCE SOL**
3.11b

George Washington

George Washington was born in Virginia in 1732. At that time, the United States was not a nation. Virginia was one of 13 colonies ruled by Great Britain, as England had become known.

Fighting for Freedom

Washington became one of the leaders of Virginia. Over time, he and other colonists grew angry with Britain. They felt that the British government treated them unfairly.

In 1775, the colonists began fighting a war to break free from Britain. They wanted to start their own nation. This fighting began the American Revolution. In a **revolution**, people fight for a change in government. Washington led the colonists' fight for freedom. The colonists won the war. The United States was a free country.

① What were the colonists fighting for in the American Revolution?

_____

_____

_____

_____

② Underline the definition of the word *revolution*.

③ Study the time line. Did George Washington become President before or after the Constitution was written?

_____

Becoming the First President

The American Revolution begins

1775

George Washington

The First President

After the war, Washington helped form a government for the new nation. In 1788, the Constitution of the United States was approved. The Constitution stated how the national government should work.

The Constitution set up a **republican form of government** for the United States. In this kind of government, people govern themselves. They choose their own leaders. In turn, the leaders make decisions and laws for the people.

Americans chose George Washington as their first President. As President, Washington helped defend the basic principles that formed the foundation of our republican form of government. A *foundation* is the basic idea used to create something. Washington earned the title "the Father of Our Country."

TextWork

4 What did George Washington do after the American Revolution?

_____

_____

_____

5 Circle the text that gives the meaning of republican form of government.

6 (Focus Skill) Why do you think George Washington is called "the Father of Our Country"?

_____

_____

_____

Led by Washington, the American troops defeat Great Britain

Washington becomes the first U.S. President

1783   1787

1789

The United States Constitution is written

Thomas Jefferson

Thomas Jefferson was born in Virginia in 1743. At an early age, he showed a love of learning. He attended college and studied to become a lawyer. Later, Jefferson became a wealthy landowner.

The Declaration of Independence

Jefferson had talents as a thinker and a writer. These talents made him an important leader at the time of the American Revolution.

In 1776, Jefferson and other leaders of the colonies met in Philadelphia, Pennsylvania. They wrote a statement listing reasons the colonists wanted independence from Britain. **Independence** is freedom from another country's control.

TextWork

7 Circle two talents that Jefferson had.

8 Underline the meaning of the word *independence*.

9 What do you think was the purpose of writing the Declaration of Independence?

_____

_____

_____

Thomas Jefferson wrote the Declaration of Independence with Benjamin Franklin and John Adams.

Thomas Jefferson lived in a home called Monticello, near Charlottesville, Virginia.

The group chose Jefferson to be the main writer of the statement. This statement is called the Declaration of Independence.

The Declaration of Independence stated that the colonies no longer belonged to Great Britain. They were now states in a new country, the United States of America. Jefferson wrote that all people have the right to "Life, Liberty, and the pursuit of Happiness." On July 4, 1776, the leaders of the 13 colonies approved the Declaration of Independence.

The Third President

In 1801, Thomas Jefferson became the third President of the United States. He served two terms as President. He died on July 4, 1826, on the fiftieth birthday of the country he had helped start.

TextWork

10 When was the Declaration of Independence approved?

_____

Jefferson's early draft of the Declaration of Independence

Abraham Lincoln

TextWork

11 Circle three jobs that Lincoln had before becoming President.

12 Underline the main cause of the American Civil War.

13 How was the idea of slavery in the Northern and Southern states different?

_____

_____

_____

During the early 1800s, Abraham Lincoln grew up working on farms. However, he became a lawyer and a leader in his state government. His excellent speaking skills made people pay attention.

The Sixteenth President

In 1861, Abraham Lincoln became President. In that same year, Northern states and Southern states began fighting a civil war. In a **civil war**, groups of people in the same country fight one another.

The Civil War began mainly over slavery. **Slavery** is the practice of forcing people to work without pay. In Southern states, farmers depended on enslaved African Americans. In Northern states, slavery was against the law. Many people in the North wanted it to be against the law in all states.

Abraham Lincoln was known for his excellent speaking skills.

The United States was so divided over the issue of equality that it split apart. The Southern states started their own country, the Confederate States of America. In the Civil War, the Confederate states fought the Union, or the United States. President Lincoln wanted to keep the country united. However, he also wanted to end slavery.

One of Lincoln's famous hats

The End of Slavery

The Civil War ended in 1865. The Union had won the war. The Confederate states again became part of the United States. Slavery was now against the law in all states. Lincoln had helped free enslaved African Americans.

Abraham Lincoln was a great President. In 2009, Americans celebrated the *Abraham Lincoln Bicentennial*. That year marked his two-hundredth birthday. Americans held events across the country to honor his life.

 **TextWork**

⑭ Underline the issue that divided Americans so much that the country split apart.

⑮ What was an important effect of the Civil War?

_____

_____

A statue of Lincoln inside the Lincoln Memorial

1. **SUMMARIZE** How did Washington, Jefferson, and Lincoln defend American principles?

_____

_____

_____

2. Write a sentence about George Washington, using the term **republican form of government**.

_____

_____

_____

3. What do you think was Abraham Lincoln's greatest achievement?

_____

_____

_____

Circle the letter of the correct answer.

4. What happened on July 4, 1776?

   A George Washington was born.

   B The Declaration of Independence was approved.

   C The Constitution of the United States was approved.

   D The Civil War began.

Draw a line connecting each person on the left with the correct achievement on the right.

5. George Washington

6. Thomas Jefferson

7. Abraham Lincoln

helped free enslaved African Americans

was the main writer of the Declaration of Independence

was the first President of the United States

Early Presidents on U.S. coins

activity

🖌 **Make a Time Line** Make a time line of important events in this lesson. Include entries for Washington, Jefferson, and Lincoln.

Working for Equal Rights

This memorial in Richmond, Virginia, honors equal rights.

THE LEGAL SYSTEM CAN FORCE OPEN DOOR
EVEN KNOCK DOWN WALLS. BUT IT CANN
THAT JOB BELONGS TO YOU A ME.
JUST

In the 1950s, more Americans began to work for equal rights. They wanted all people to be treated fairly under the law. Thurgood Marshall, Rosa Parks, Dr. Martin Luther King, Jr., and César Chávez all worked for equal rights. **Think about how these Americans worked for equal rights.**

Essential Question
✓ How did American citizens work to defend American principles?

SOL HISTORY AND SOCIAL SCIENCE SOL
3.11b

Marshall (center) posed outside the Supreme Court in 1954.

TextWork

1 What job did Marshall have after graduation?

_____

_____

2 Circle the name of the most important court in the United States.

3 What does this court do?

_____

_____

_____

Thurgood Marshall

Thurgood Marshall was born in Maryland in 1908. As a young man, he tried to enter a law school. However, he was not allowed to attend. Like other African Americans at the time, he did not have equal rights. This unfair treatment did not stop Marshall. He attended another law school and graduated.

Defending Rights

As a lawyer, Marshall worked to defend people's rights. His most famous court case was decided by the United States Supreme Court in 1954. This court is the most important court in the United States. It decides whether a law agrees with the Constitution of the United States.

At that time, African American children in some parts of the country could not go to the same public schools as white children. Marshall and many others believed this was unfair. They also believed it was against the Constitution.

The Supreme Court agreed with Marshall. The court decided that African American and white children should be allowed to attend the same schools.

Marshall talked with a group of students.

Supreme Court Justice

In 1967, President Lyndon Johnson chose Marshall to serve as a **justice**, or judge, on the Supreme Court. Marshall became the first African American Supreme Court justice. As a justice, he continued to help protect African Americans and other people from unequal treatment. Marshall served on the Supreme Court for 24 years.

 **TextWork**

❹ Scan the text on this page. Circle the sentence that explains how the Supreme Court agreed with Marshall's ideas.

❺ Underline the important event in African American history that took place in 1967.

Marshall and his family prepared for his ceremony to become a new Supreme Court justice.

Rosa Parks

Rosa Parks was another African American who worked for equal rights. She was born in Alabama in 1913. She later lived in Montgomery, Alabama.

A Seat on a Bus

In some places in the 1950s, African Americans had to sit in the back of public buses. They could sit in the middle only if no white people wanted the seats.

In 1955, Parks had worked a long, hard day. She was a seamstress at a department store in Montgomery. She boarded a public bus to go home. After paying the fare, she sat in a middle seat of the bus. Three other African Americans sat next to her.

Parks (below) helped bring changes to unfair bus laws.

TextWork

6 Where did Rosa Parks live?

_____

_____

7 Underline the text that describes the rules for riding public buses in some places in the 1950s.

In 1999, Parks received the Congressional Gold Medal. It is the highest honor the United States Congress can give to a citizen.

Soon seats at the front of the bus filled up. The bus driver told Parks and the three other African Americans to move to the back of the bus. The others did, but Parks refused. The driver called police, and Parks was arrested.

The Montgomery Bus Boycott

After Parks's arrest, African Americans began a boycott of buses in Montgomery. During a **boycott**, people refuse to buy or use something. The boycott caused the bus company to lose a lot of money.

After almost a year, the Supreme Court said that making African Americans sit separately from white people was against the Constitution of the United States. Rosa Parks had helped bring changes to laws so that all people would have equal rights.

TextWork

8 (Focus Skill) Why do you think Parks refused to move to the back of the bus?

_____

_____

9 What happened in the Montgomery bus boycott?

_____

_____

10 Underline the text that describes the change that Rosa Parks helped bring.

Dr. Martin Luther King, Jr.

Dr. Martin Luther King, Jr., was an African American minister. He believed that laws should treat all people equally and give them the same rights.

Working for Equality

Dr. King was born in Atlanta, Georgia, in 1929. Growing up, he saw that African Americans did not have the same rights as other Americans. Laws often separated African Americans from others.

At college, Dr. King developed strong public-speaking skills. He used those skills to work for his dream of equality. He spoke against unfair laws and led marches. Instead of fighting, Dr. King used peaceful actions to work for equality. He did not want people to hurt others.

A Dream for Equality

TextWork

11 What job did Dr. King have?

_____

_____

12 Underline the ways Dr. King worked for equality.

Dr. King (center) led marches in support of civil rights.

Dr. King gave many speeches. His most famous is titled "I Have a Dream." In the speech, Dr. King said, "I have a dream that one day this nation will rise up and live out the true meaning of its creed: 'We hold these truths to be self-evident; that all men are created equal.'"

New Civil Rights Laws

In 1964, the United States government passed a new law to support civil rights. **Civil rights** are the rights that give everyone equal treatment under the law. The new law said that all Americans have the right to use public places and services.

In 1964, Dr. King won the Nobel Peace Prize for his work. Nobel Prizes are given to people who make important contributions. Dr. King is remembered for helping bring about changes in laws through peaceful actions.

TextWork

⓭ What was the title of Dr. King's most famous speech?

_____

_____

⓮ Underline the definition of the term *civil rights*.

⓯ Circle the text that tells what Dr. King is remembered for.

After signing the Civil Rights Bill in 1964, President Johnson shook Dr. King's hand.

NAT·
MDCCC
XXXIII
OB·
MDCCC
XCVI

ALFR·
NOBEL

A Nobel Prize medal

Chávez gave speeches to gain support for farm worker's rights.

César Chávez

César Chávez was a Mexican American who worked to improve conditions for farm workers. When he was born in 1927, his family was facing hard times. The Chávezes were migrant (MY•gruhnt), or traveling, farm workers.

Chávez's family moved from farm to farm, picking fruits and vegetables. Like other migrant workers, the Chávezes were always traveling around to find work.

Working for Change

As an adult, Chávez remembered the hardships his family and other Mexican Americans faced. In 1958, he became the leader of the Community Service Organization, or CSO. This group worked to gain civil rights for Hispanic Americans.

16 (Focus Skill) How was life hard for César Chávez's family and other migrant workers?

_____

_____

_____

_____

In 1962, Chávez helped form a group that later became known as the United Farm Workers. This group worked for higher pay and better working conditions for migrant workers.

Peaceful Action

Like Dr. King, Chávez did not believe in violence. He organized peaceful actions to help the workers. He held public hunger strikes in which he did not eat for many days. These hunger strikes brought attention to the lives of the workers.

César Chávez died in 1993. More than 50,000 people came to his funeral. A year later, President Bill Clinton honored Chávez with the Presidential Medal of Freedom. This medal is awarded to people who make important contributions.

 **TextWork**

⓱ Underline the text that explains how Chávez worked to improve the lives of farm workers.

⓲ Circle the text that tells how Chávez was like Dr. King.

A United Farm Workers patch

Children in History

Jessica Govea

In 1947, Jessica Govea was born into a hardworking Mexican American family in California. By the age of four, she was working in the cotton fields. Jessica helped her father set up meetings for the CSO. She later became the president of the Junior CSO. With other children who were farm workers, she persuaded community leaders to build a park. Before she was 20, she joined the United Farm Workers. She organized boycotts that led farm owners to treat their workers better.

Make It Relevant **What are some ways you can help your community?**

1. **SUMMARIZE** How have citizens worked to defend American principles?

_____

_____

_____

2. How are the words *courts* and **justice** related?

_____

_____

_____

3. How did Thurgood Marshall's personal experiences lead him to work for equality?

_____

_____

4. Do you think Rosa Parks chose the best way to change unfair laws? Explain your answer.

_____

_____

_____

Draw a line connecting the person on the left with his or her achievement on the right.

5. Rosa Parks

held hunger strikes to help migrant workers

6. César Chávez

caused a bus boycott that led to changes in unfair laws

7. Dr. Martin Luther King, Jr.

won the Nobel Peace Prize in 1964

writing

✎ **Create a Radio Interview** With a partner, write an interview for a person in this lesson. One partner will ask the questions, and the other will answer for the person. Tape-record the interview, and play it for the class.

A Presidential Medal of Freedom

Honoring Our Nation's Heroes

Many people have fought to protect our country's freedoms. Americans have two special days to remember **veterans**, or those who have served in the military. These special days are Veterans Day and Memorial Day. **Think about why Americans show respect for veterans on Veterans Day and Memorial Day.**

The Korean War Veterans Memorial in Washington, D.C.

Essential Question
✔ Why do we recognize Veterans Day and Memorial Day?

 HISTORY AND SOCIAL SCIENCE SOL
3.11c

TextWork

1 Underline the purpose of Veterans Day.

2 When is Veterans Day observed?

_____

_____

3 Why do you think the name *Armistice Day* was changed to Veterans Day?

_____

_____

_____

_____

Veterans Day

Veterans Day is a day when we honor Americans who have served in the military. It is a time to show our respect for them. It is a time to remember all they have done to keep our country free. Veterans Day is observed each year in November.

Veterans Day began as Armistice Day in 1919. An *armistice* is an agreement to end a war. President Woodrow Wilson started this holiday to celebrate the end of World War I. He said, "Armistice Day will be filled with solemn pride in the heroism of those who died in the country's service."

On Veterans Day, Americans honor all veterans. They honor those who fought and died in battles. They also honor those who served in times of peace. People celebrate Veterans Day with flag-raisings, parades, and speeches.

Veterans wear their uniforms proudly and take part in parades.

The Tomb of the Unknowns in Arlington, Virginia

Memorial Day

Memorial Day is a day to recognize and show respect to Americans who died in wars while serving their country. It takes place each year in May.

Memorial Day began after the Civil War. It was first known as Decoration Day. People decorated the graves of soldiers who had died in the war. In 1868, an army general declared Decoration Day a national holiday. A **national holiday** is a day for remembering an important person, idea, or event in the nation's history.

Today, on Memorial Day, people still visit cemeteries to remember those who died for their nation. They bring flowers and American flags for soldiers' graves. Some communities organize Memorial Day parades and picnics.

 TextWork

❹ Whom does Memorial Day honor?

_____

_____

❺ Underline the text that tells when Memorial Day takes place.

❻ How can the two words that make up the term *national holiday* help you remember its meaning?

_____

_____

_____

Other National Holidays

People in the United States celebrate their American heritage on many different national holidays. A **heritage** is a set of values and ways of life handed down from people who lived long ago.

Celebrating People

For example, people celebrate the birthday of Dr. Martin Luther King, Jr., each January. This holiday honors his peaceful actions for civil rights.

Presidents' Day is celebrated in February. This holiday once marked the birthday of George Washington. Today, we honor all United States Presidents on this day.

In October, Columbus Day recognizes Christopher Columbus's arrival in the Americas. Many people also celebrate American Indian culture on this holiday.

❼ Underline the definition of the word *heritage*.

❽ How does your family celebrate its heritage?

_____

_____

_____

_____

❾ Scan the text on these two pages. Circle the names of two national holidays.

Americans celebrate Independence Day in different ways.

Celebrating History

National holidays celebrate important events in history, too. Our first leaders signed the Declaration of Independence on July 4, 1776. Every Fourth of July, we celebrate Independence Day. On this day, people watch parades and fireworks. Some fly the American flag or wear its colors.

On September 17, 1787, the leaders of the United States signed the Constitution. To honor this event, many people celebrate Constitution Day on September 17.

In 1863, President Abraham Lincoln chose the last Thursday in November as Thanksgiving Day. Many people think of a festival that happened in the fall of 1621 as the first Thanksgiving. Then, English settlers gathered with the American Indians who had helped them. Together, they gave thanks for a good first harvest.

TextWork

10 Why is the Fourth of July important to Americans?

_____

_____

_____

11 What historical event do people remember on Thanksgiving Day?

_____

_____

_____

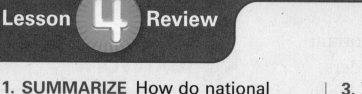

1. **SUMMARIZE** How do national holidays celebrate the soldiers who protected our country's freedoms?

_____

_____

_____

2. Who are **veterans**?

_____

_____

_____

3. What is the difference between Memorial Day and Veterans Day?

_____

_____

_____

Circle the letter of the correct answer.

4. A holiday celebrated in May is—

   A Presidents' Day

   B Columbus Day

   C Veterans Day

   D Memorial Day

Draw a line connecting each holiday on the left with the month in which it is observed on the right.

5. Independence Day   in November

6. Veterans Day   in May

7. Memorial Day   in July

activity

🖍 **Make a Poster** Imagine that you are in charge of your community's Memorial Day celebration. Make a poster that tells about the events and activities you have planned.

A patriotic ribbon

People Serving Others

Lesson 5

These people are building a new home for a family in need.

Virginia's citizens have many ways to take an active part in serving their community, state, and nation. Think about how people might help their community, state, and nation.

Essential Question

✓ How do people serve their community, state, and nation?

HISTORY AND SOCIAL SCIENCE SOL
3.11d

At voting booths, people can vote in private. **EIP**

TextWork

❶ Underline the text that explains the meaning of the word *responsibility*.

❷ How does voting allow a person to serve?

_____

_____

_____

❸ Study the photograph. Why is each voter standing alone at a voting booth?

_____

_____

_____

Citizens Have Duties

For every right, there is a responsibility. A **responsibility** is a duty. It is something a person should do because it is necessary or important. Voting, for example, is both a right and a responsibility.

Voting

Voting is one way that people can serve their community, state, or nation. Voting allows citizens to make choices in their government. By voting, citizens elect, or choose, their government's leaders.

Many people go to special voting places on election day. An **election** is a time set aside for voting. Voters mark their choices on a ballot. A **ballot** lists all the possible choices in an election. Each vote is kept secret. Only the results are announced.

Good Citizens

Good citizens also **cooperate**, or work together. They can cooperate at the local, state, and national levels.

Students are being good citizens when they show respect for their classmates and teachers. Students should follow rules, do their best work, and take part in class.

Good citizens take part in all levels of government. Adults may run for office and serve in their government. Good citizens keep up with important issues. They go to meetings and give their opinions.

Good citizens may also serve their nation by joining the military. They can join the Army, Navy, Air Force, or Marine Corps. As members of the military, they help protect our country's freedoms.

TextWork

❹ Circle two ways a citizen can serve his or her community, state, or nation.

❺ (Focus Skill) How would you describe a good citizen?

_____

_____

_____

_____

People running for office tell their opinions about important issues to voters.

Helping Others

TextWork

❻ Circle the definition of the term *common good*.

❼ What are some ways people can volunteer?

_____

_____

_____

_____

Volunteering is an important way to serve your community, state, and nation.

Good citizens work for the **common good**, or the good of everyone. They do this by solving problems together. Responsible citizens share ideas to find ways to improve their community.

Helping others is another way to work for the common good. Many volunteers help people in need. **Volunteers** are people who choose to work without getting paid.

People can volunteer in their community, state, and nation. Some volunteers work on community projects. They collect food and clothes for people in need. Other volunteers work at hospitals and schools. They spend time with patients, or they help students learn. Still other volunteers help protect the environment. They clean up parks or along rivers and lakes.

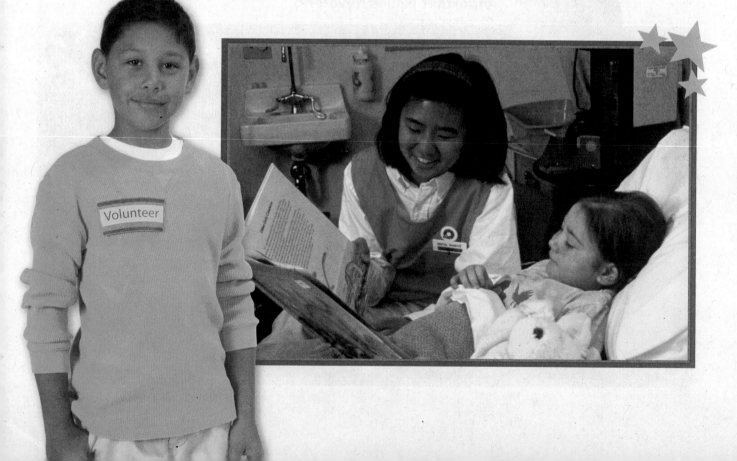

A jury has a responsibility to make careful decisions.

Other Responsibilities

Citizens of the United States do not have to vote or help others. They have a choice. However, the law does require citizens to do certain things.

Citizens must obey laws and pay taxes. Laws help keep order and people safe. Taxes allow the government to provide services. Citizens must also serve on a jury if called upon to do so. A **jury** is a group of people who meet to decide whether a person has broken a law.

People who do not obey the laws must face the consequences. A **consequence** (KAHN•suh•kwens) is something that happens because of what a person does. For example, if someone disobeys a traffic law, one consequence might be a car accident. A person who breaks a law may have to pay a fine or spend time in jail.

TextWork

❽ Circle the responsibilities of citizens that are required by law.

❾ Underline the text that tells the job of a person who serves on a jury.

❿ (Focus Skill) What might be the consequences of stealing?

_____

_____

_____

_____

1. **SUMMARIZE** What important responsibilities do citizens have?

_____

_____

_____

2. Use the words **responsibility** and **jury** in a sentence.

_____

_____

_____

3. How do citizens choose their government leaders?

_____

_____

_____

4. What are some ways people can volunteer?

_____

_____

_____

Draw a line connecting each action on the left with the correct possible consequence on the right.

5. copying another student's test answers

6. crossing the street on a "Don't Walk" signal

7. helping build a home for a family in need

getting hit by a car

helping the common good

breaking the teacher's trust

writing

Write a Report Write a short report that tells ways to be a responsible citizen.

The Smiths volunteered to clean a highway in Virginia.

Most people in the United States, or their families, have come from many places around the world. Even so, we are united as Americans. **Think about all the places Americans come from and all the things that unite us.**

The Statue of Liberty in New York Harbor

Essential Questions

✓ What unites the people of the United States?
✓ What are some benefits of diversity in the United States?

 HISTORY AND SOCIAL SCIENCE SOL
3.12

❶ Use the word *diverse* in a sentence.

_____

_____

_____

_____

❷ Underline the definition of the term *ethnic group*.

❸ Study the circle graph. Which world region do most Americans born outside the United States come from?

_____

A Diverse People

People in the United States are **diverse**, or different from one another. They have different origins, or backgrounds. They or earlier members of their families have come from different places.

Because of this, Americans represent many ethnic groups. An **ethnic group** is made up of people from the same country or with a shared way of life. Each ethnic group brings some of its culture to the United States. Each group has its own holidays. It has special kinds of food, clothing, and music.

Each ethnic group has its own customs, too. A **custom** is a way of doing something. For example, it is a custom in the United States to greet someone by shaking hands. In Japan, people greet others by bowing. Different customs make our nation diverse.

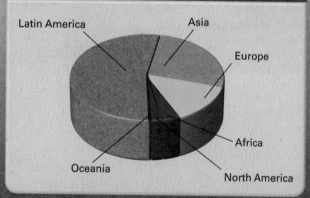

Origins of Americans Born Outside the United States

Latin America
Asia
Europe
Africa
North America
Oceania

Americans share special kinds of music and dance.

The Benefits of Diversity

Living in a country with such diversity, or differences, has benefits. Walking down the streets of most cities, people can enjoy the smells of different kinds of foods, such as Chinese, Mexican, or Italian. They might see other people dressed in traditional clothing. They can listen to the many kinds of music that ethnic groups have brought to the United States.

People have many ways to learn about other cultures. One way is by reading literature written by people from other cultures. A writer often tells about his or her culture in stories and poems.

People can also learn about other cultures through music, dance, art, and architecture. Religious traditions are also an important part of culture. People can see these cultural traditions at museums and festivals.

TextWork

❹ (Focus Skill) Why does the Unite
States have cultural diversit

_____

_____

_____

_____

❺ Underline the benefits of diversity.

❻ Circle some ways people can learn about other cultures.

Americans enjoy many different kinds of foods.

Americans may dress in traditional clothing.

United by Basic Principles

The United States is a nation of great diversity. People may speak different languages. They may eat different foods or follow different religions. Yet they are united. They are united as Americans by the shared basic principles of a republican form of government. These ideas help shape our nation and its representative democracy.

Equality Under the Law

Americans are united by the principle of equality under the law. They share a respect for the rights and freedoms of every individual, or person. They believe in the idea that everyone deserves to be treated fairly.

8 Underline the text that describes the principle of equality under the law.

This photograph from 1939 shows people taking part in a ceremony to become citizens of the United States.

Today, people still become new citizens of the United States.

Life, Liberty, and the Pursuit of Happiness

Americans are also united by individual rights to life, liberty, and the pursuit of happiness. Having these rights has attracted many people to the United States.

Some people have come because they were in danger in their own countries. They have fled war or bad treatment by the government in their homeland.

Many newcomers gain more freedoms in the United States than they had before. Here, they can follow any religion. They are free to speak and write their opinions.

Most people move to the United States for new opportunities. They hope to make a better life here. For them, the United States is a land of opportunity. A person who works hard can be a success.

 TextWork

9 Circle three rights that unite the citizens of the United States.

10 Why do most people move to the United States?

_____

_____

_____

_____

Patriotism

TextWork

⓫ Underline the definition of the word *patriotism*.

⓬ What are some ways Americans show patriotism?

_____

_____

_____

_____

As Americans, we are proud of our nation. We show our **patriotism**, or love of country. Together, we are all Americans.

Americans have many ways to show patriotism. Many people recite *The Pledge of Allegiance* and sing "The Star-Spangled Banner." Many people also celebrate holidays that honor our nation. They put up monuments to help remember the people and events that have shaped our nation. For example, the Washington Monument in Washington, D.C., honors George Washington, our first President.

These citizens show their patriotism by celebrating Constitution Day.

1. **SUMMARIZE** How are the people of the United States both diverse and united?

_____

_____

_____

2. Write a description of a community that is **diverse**.

_____

_____

3. What have different ethnic groups brought to the United States?

_____

_____

_____

4. What basic principles unite American citizens?

_____

_____

Draw a line connecting each word on the left with the correct definition on the right.

5. diverse   a way of doing something

6. custom   love of country

7. patriotism   different from one another

writing

✎ **Write a Diary Entry** Write a diary entry as if you are moving to the United States. Explain why you want to become an American citizen. Explain how your reason for moving might be different from others who move.

An old Russian passport

Picture Clues

VOCABULARY

This crossword puzzle is complete, but which picture clues match the puzzle words? Draw a line connecting each word to its clue. One is done for you.

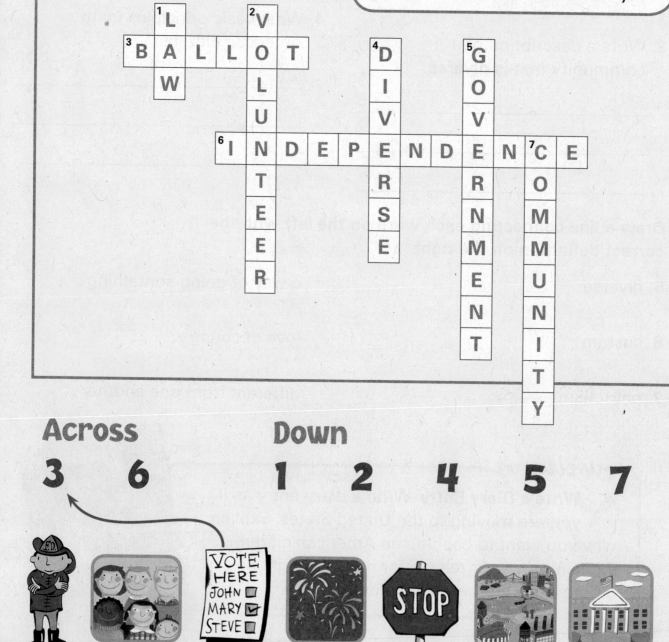

Across
3   6

Down
1   2   4   5   7

If They'd Had the Internet

Which famous people from this unit might have written these e-mails? Write each person's name.

From: _____
To: southernstates@csa.com
Subject: The Civil War

I want the Southern states to rejoin the United States. I also want to end slavery.

From: _____
To: leaders@13colonies.com
Subject: First Draft of the Declaration

Please review my first draft of the Declaration of Independence. I'd like to get it approved by July 4, 1776.

From: _____
To: government@britain.com
Subject: Leading the Fight for Freedom

The colonists and I feel that the British government treats us unfairly. As a result, I'll lead the fight for our freedom.

Good Citizens

These four good citizens made a difference. What are their names?

I did not give up my seat on the bus and was arrested. That helped change unfair laws.

_____

I worked to improve conditions for farm workers.

_____

I used peaceful actions to work for equality for all people. I won the Nobel Prize in 1964.

_____

I worked for people's equal rights. I was the first African American Supreme Court justice.

_____

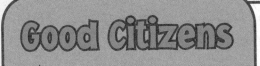

Review and Test Prep

Unit 6

The Big Idea

The American people are united by common beliefs and experiences.

Summarize the Unit

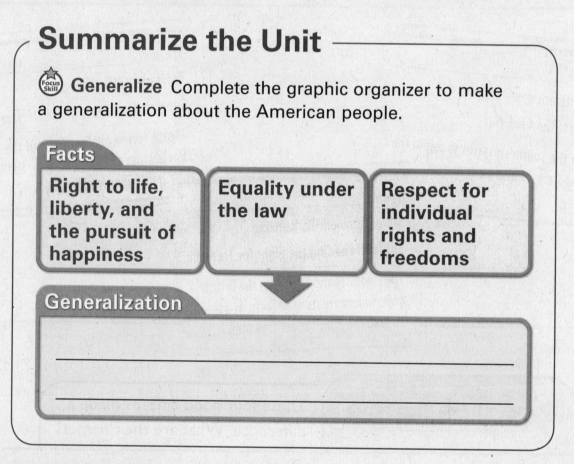

Focus Skill **Generalize** Complete the graphic organizer to make a generalization about the American people.

Facts

| Right to life, liberty, and the pursuit of happiness | Equality under the law | Respect for individual rights and freedoms |

Generalization

_____

_____

Use Vocabulary

Complete each sentence with a vocabulary term from the Word Bank.

1. A government serves its _____.

2. Americans are a _____ people.

3. _____ need many things to run smoothly.

4. The United States government is a _____.

5. _____ are important rules.

Word Bank

communities p. 223

laws p. 224

citizens p. 225

republican form of government p. 231

civil right p. 243

diverse p. 260

Think About It

Circle the letter of the correct answer.

6. What is a group of people who make laws, carry out laws, and decide if laws have been broken?

   A Business

   B Government

   C State

   D Nation

7. What tells people what they must or must not do?

   F Rule

   G Right

   H Principle

   J Freedom

8.
   - to keep people safe
   - to keep order

   These statements describe the purpose of—

   A principles and decisions

   B choices and benefits

   C rules and laws

   D rights and freedoms

9. Which is a purpose of government?

   F To make people volunteer

   G To serve on juries

   H To make laws

   J To pay taxes

10. "...Life, Liberty, and the pursuit of Happiness."

    This quote lists the rights in the United States held by—

    A all citizens

    B most citizens

    C citizens who are older than 18

    D citizens who are older than 65

11. What is the principle of equality under the law?

    F People can gather in groups.

    G All people are treated fairly.

    H People can choose their rights.

    J All people can read anything.

12.

This person—

A was the first United States President

B wrote the Declaration of Independence

C was a Supreme Court justice

D helped free enslaved African Americans

13. The Constitution of the United States set up a—

F state form of government

G republican monarchy

H democratic monarchy

J republican form of government

14. Who was the main writer of the Declaration of Independence?

A John Adams

B Thomas Jefferson

C Abraham Lincoln

D George Washington

15. Before the Civil War, what issue divided the United States?

F Slavery in Northern states

G The end of slavery

H Disagreements over borders

J Equality for all people

16.

This person helped free enslaved African Americans.

This sentence describes—

A John Adams

B Thomas Jefferson

C Abraham Lincoln

D George Washington

17. Who served as a justice of the United States Supreme Court?

F César Chávez

G Dr. Martin Luther King, Jr.

H Thurgood Marshall

J Rosa Parks

18.

This person's actions—

A caused a boycott of buses in Montgomery, Alabama

B earned a Nobel Peace Prize

C helped migrant farm workers

D allowed all children to attend the same schools

19. Both César Chávez and Dr. Martin Luther King, Jr.,—

F were lawyers

G used peaceful actions

H were migrant workers

J held government jobs

20. Which holiday honors Americans who died serving their country?

A Independence Day

B Memorial Day

C Presidents' Day

D Veterans Day

21. Which day is observed in November?

F Independence Day

G Memorial Day

H Presidents' Day

J Veterans Day

22. Which is a benefit of diversity?

    A Living by shared principles

    B Following rules of citizenship

    C Learning about other cultures

    D Helping people in need

23. Which helps unite all American citizens?

    F The respect for individual rights and freedoms

    G The practice of religious traditions

    H The enjoyment of different art and music

    J The beliefs of different ethnic groups

24.

Year	Population of Virginia
2000	7,000,000 people
2005	7,300,000 people
2010	8,000,000 people

Which generalization about Virginia's population is correct?

    A It increased.

    B It decreased.

    C It increased and then decreased.

    D It decreased and then increased.

Answer these questions.

25. Why is government necessary?

_____

_____

26. Give two examples of citizens who have defended the principles of American government.

_____

_____

27. What makes American citizens a diverse people?

_____

_____

It's a busy day in Eco's town. Today is Election Day, and if the election runs smoothly, the town will celebrate at the Citizens' Fair. If you can keep everything running smoothly, you'll earn a golden fair ticket! Go online to play the game now.

HMH

ECO

Show What You Know

Writing Write "Who Am I?" Statements

Choose a person from this unit who defended basic American principles. Write at least three "Who Am I?" statements about the person. Then read the statements to your classmates to see whether they can guess whom you wrote about.

Activity Make a Citizenship Handbook

Make a handbook that tells how to be a good citizen. List the responsibilities of citizens. Describe different ways people can serve their community, state, and nation. Include examples of people who have helped the common good.

For Your Reference

Glossary

The Glossary contains important history and social science words and their definitions, listed in alphabetical order. Each word is respelled as it would be in a dictionary. When you see this mark ´ after a syllable, pronounce that syllable with more force. The page number at the end of the definition tells where the word is used in this book. Guide words at the top of each page help you quickly locate the word you need to find.

add, āce, câre, pälm; end, ēqual; it, īce; odd, ōpen, ôrder; tŏŏk, pōōl; up, bûrn; yōō as *u* in *fuse*; oil; pout; ə as *a* in *above*, *e* in *sicken*, *i* in *possible*, *o* in *melon*, *u* in *circus*; check; ring; thin; this; zh as in *vision*

achievement (ə•chēv´mənt) The reaching of a goal through hard work. p. 158

adapt (ə•dapt´) To change to fit the surroundings. p. 16

aerial view (ar´•ē•əl vyü) A view from above. p. I[1]

agriculture (a´gri•kəl•chər) Farming, including the growing of crops and the raising of farm animals. p. 56

ancient (ānk´shənt) A time very long ago. p. 9

aqueduct (a´kwə•dəkt) A human-made pipeline or channel used to carry water to a city. p. 68

architecture (är´kə•tek•chər) A style of building. p. 28

ballot (ba´lət) A list of choices in an election. p. 254

barter (bär´tər) To trade goods or services without using money. p. 101

benefit (be´nə•fit) To get something good. p. 200

boycott (boi´kät) A time when people refuse to buy or use something. p. 241

budget (bə´jət) A plan for spending and saving money. p. 207

capital resource (ka´pə•təl rē´sôrs) A good, such as a machine, tool, or building, that is made by people and used to produce other goods and services. p. 21

caravan (kar´ə•van) A group of traders who travel together. p. 110

cardinal direction (kärd´nəl də•rek´shən) One of the four main directions—north, south, east, and west. p. 184

category (ka´tə•gōr•ē) A group of things that are alike in some way. p. 47

cause (kôz) Something that makes something else happen. p. 87

characteristic (kar•ik•tə•ris´tik) A different trait. p. 12

citizen (si´tə•zən) A person who lives in a community, state, or nation. p. 225

civil rights (si´vəl rīts) Rights that give everyone equal treatment under the law. p. 243

civil war (si´vəl wôr) A war in which groups of people in the same country fight one another. p. 234

civilization (si•və•lə•zā´shən) A large group of people living in an organized way. p. 27

claim (klām) To say that you own something. p. 134

classify (kla´sə•fī) To sort things into categories. p. 47

climate (klī´mət) The weather a place has over a long period of time. p. 13

colony (kä´lə•nē) A settlement ruled by a country that is far away. p. 136

colonize (kä´lə•nīz) To set up a colony. p. 148

column (kä´ləm) A support for a building's roof. p. 29

common good (kä´mən good) The good of everyone. p. 256

community (kə•myoo´nə•tē) A place where people live, work, and play. pp. 13, 223

compare (kəm•par´) To tell how things are alike. p. 127

compass rose (kəm´pəs rōz) A drawing on a map that shows directions. p. I5

conclusion (kən•kloo´zhən) A general statement about an idea. p. 175

conflict (kän´flikt) A disagreement between people. p. 143

conquer (kän´kər) To take over. p. 104

consequence (kän´sə•kwens) Something that happens because of what a person does. p. 257

constitution (kän•stə•too´shən) A written set of laws that tell how a government will work. p. 227

consumer (kän•soo´mər) A person who buys a product or service. p. 197

continent (kän´tə•nənt) One of the seven largest land areas on Earth. pp. I2, 178

contrast (kän´trast) To tell how things are different. p. 127

contribution (kän•trə•byoo´shən) The act of giving or doing something. p. 28

cooperate (kō•ä´pə•rāt) To work together. p. 255

crossroads (krôs´ rōdz) A place with a central location. p. 108

culture (kul´chər) A way of life shared by members of a group. p. 64

custom (kəs´təm) A way of doing something. p. 260

D

democracy (di•mä´krə•sē) A government in which citizens make the decisions by voting. p. 31

desert (de´zərt) A place where the climate is dry. p. 90

detail (dē´tāl) More information about the main idea of a paragraph. p. 7

direct democracy (də•rekt´ di•mä´krə•sē) A government in which people vote to make their own rules and laws. p. 31

diverse (di•vərs´) Different from one another. p. 260

E

economic choice (e•kə•nä´mik chois) A decision among alternatives or possibilities about earning, spending, or saving money. p. 204

economy (i•kä´nə•mē) The way a community, state, or country makes and uses goods and services. p. 196

effect (i•fekt´) Something that happens as a result of a cause. p. 87

election (i•lek´shən) A time set aside for voting. p. 254

empire (em´pīr) All the land and people under the control of a powerful nation. p. 62

environment (in•vī´rən•mənt) The surroundings in which people, plants, and animals live. p. 16

equality under the law (i•kwä´lə•tē ən´dər the lô) The idea that all people are to be treated fairly. p. 226

equator (i•kwā´tər) On a map or a globe, an imaginary line around the middle of Earth that divides Earth into the Northern and Southern Hemispheres. pp. I3, 180

ethnic group (eth´nik groop) A group of people from the same country or with a shared way of life. p. 260

GLOSSARY

GLOSSARY

European (yûr•ə•pē´ən) A person from one of the countries of Europe. p. 130

expedition (ek•spə•di´shən) A trip for a purpose. p. 142

explorer (ik•splôr´ər) A person who travels seeking new discoveries. p. 130

Fall Line (fôl līn) An area where the height of land changes suddenly and causes rivers to form rapids or waterfalls. p. 154

generalize (jen´rə•līz) To make a general statement about a group of ideas. p. 221

generation (je•nə•rā´shən) The time between the birth of parents and the birth of their children. p. 102

globe (glōb) A model of Earth. p. I[1]

good (good) Something that people make or use to satisfy needs and wants. p. 20

government (gə´vərn•mənt) A group of people who make rules and laws, carry out rules and laws, and decide if rules and laws have been broken. pp. 28, 224

grid system (grid sis´təm) A set of lines the same distance apart that divides a map into small boxes. p. 185

griot (grē´ō) A West African storyteller who passes on his or her culture's history. p. 102

H

hemisphere (he´mə•sfir) Half of a sphere, or globe, created by the prime meridian or equator. pp. I3, 180

heritage (her´ə•tij) A set of values and ways of life handed down from people who lived earlier. p. 250

human characteristic (hyoo´mən kar•ik•tə•ris´tik) A feature made by people, such as a city, farm, or road. p. 22

human resource (hyoo´mən rē´sôrs) A person working to produce a good or a service. p. 21

I

income (in´kəm) The money people are paid for their work. p. 204

independence (in•də•pen´dəns) Freedom from another's control. p. 232

inland (in´land) An area away from the coast. p. 56

inset map (in´set map) A small map within a larger map. p. I4

intermediate direction (in•tər•mē´dē•ət də•rek´shən) One of four directions—northeast, southeast, northwest, and southwest—that lie between the cardinal directions. p. 184

irrigate (ir´ə•gāt) To bring water to. p. 96

J

jury (joo´rē) A group of people who meet to decide whether a person has broken a law. p. 257

justice (jəs´təs) A judge. p. 239

L

land use (land yüs) The way most of the land in a region is used. p. 198

law (lô) An important rule that is written and carried out by the government. p. 224

legend (le´jənd) A story that may or may not be true, usually about a real person or event. p. 141

locator (lō´kā•tər) A small map or globe that shows where the place on the main map is located within a larger area. p. I4

main idea (mān ī•dē´ə) The most important idea of a paragraph. p. 7

majority rule (mə•jôr´ə•tē ro͞ol) The idea that receives the majority of the votes, or more than half of the votes, passes. p. 31

map (map) A flat drawing of a place on Earth. p. I[1]

map legend (map le´jənd) A box on a map that explains the symbols used on the map; also called a map key. p. I4

map scale (map skā´əl) A part of a map that compares a distance on the map to a distance in the real world. p. I5

map title (map tī´təl) A title that tells the subject of the map. p. I4

Memorial Day (mə•môr´ē•əl dā) A day for the recognition of and respect for Americans who died in wars while they were serving their country. It is observed in May. p. 249

modify (mä´də•fī) To change. p. 192

mosaic (mō•zā´ik) A picture made from small pieces of glass or stone. p. 30

mosque (mäsk) A house of worship for Muslims. p. 113

motivation (mō•tə•vā´shən) A reason for doing something. p. 131

mountain range (moun´tən rānj) A group of mountains. p. 52

national holiday (na´shə•nəl hä´lə•dā) A day for remembering an important person, idea, or event in a nation's history. p. 249

natural resource (na´chə•rəl rē´sôrs) Materials that come from nature, such as water, soil, wood, or coal. p. 21

oasis (ō•ā´səs) A place where a spring gives a source of water. p. 92

ocean (ō´shən) One of Earth's five largest bodies of water. p. I2

opportunity cost (ä•pər•to͞o´nə•tē kôst) The next best choice that is given up when a decision is made. p. 206

P

patriotism (pā´trē•ə•ti•zəm) The feeling of love people have for their country. p. 264

peninsula (pə•nin´sə•lə) Land that is almost completely surrounded by water. p. 12

permanent (pər´mə•nənt) Long-lasting. p. 153

physical characteristic (fi´zi•kəl kar•ik•tə•ris´tik) A feature found in nature, such as land and water. p. 12

population (pä•pyə•lā´shən) The total number of people living in a place. p. 61

preserve (pri•sərv´) To keep something from spoiling. p. 97

prime meridian (prīm mə•rid´ē•ən) On a map or a globe, an imaginary line that runs between the North Pole and the South Pole. It divides Earth into the Eastern and Western Hemispheres. p. 181

principle (prin´sə•pəl) An idea that people believe in. p. 226

producer (prə•do͞o´sər) A person who uses resources to make goods or provide services. p. 20

R

rapids (ra´pəds) Shallow, rocky areas of fast-moving water. p. 148

raw material (rô mə•tir´ē•əl) A natural resource that can be used to make goods. p. 152

GLOSSARY

GLOSSARY

region (rē´jən) A place that has common characteristics. pp. 52, 179

representative democracy (re•pri•zen´tə•tiv di•mä´krə•sē) A government in which people vote for, or elect, a smaller group of citizens to make the rules and laws for everyone. p. 70

republic (ri•pub´lik) A form of government in which citizens elect leaders to represent them. p. 70

republican form of government (ri•pə´bli•kən form əv gə´vərn•mənt) A representative democracy, or kind of government in which people govern themselves. p. 231

responsibility (ri•spän•sə•bi´lə•tē) A duty, or something a person should do because it is necessary and important. p. 254

revolution (rev•ə•lōō´shən) A fight for a change in government. p. 230

right (rīt) A freedom. p. 225

rule (rōōl) A statement that tells people what they must or must not do. p. 224

S

savanna (sə•va´nə) A grassy plain. p. 92

scarce (skers) Hard to find or get. p. 201

service (sər´vəs) Activities people do for others to satisfy their needs and wants. p. 20

slavery (slā´vər•ē) The practice of forcing people to work without pay. p. 234

specialization (spe•shə•lī•zā´shən) Focusing on producing one kind of good or service. p. 200

sponsor (spän´sər) A person or group who pays for another's activity. p. 134

T

terrace (ter´əs) A flat area dug into the side of a hill or mountain. p. 22

trade (trād) To exchange one good or service for another. p. 17

tradition (trə•dish´ən) A custom that is passed on to others. p. 103

V

veteran (ve´tə•rən) A person who has served in the military. p. 247

Veterans Day (ve´tə•rəns dā) A day for the recognition of and respect for Americans who served in the military. It is observed in November. p. 248

volunteer (vä•lən•tir´) A person who chooses to work without getting paid. p. 256

Index

The Index lets you know where information about important people, places, and events appear in the book. All key words, or entries, are listed in alphabetical order. For each entry, the page reference indicates where information about that entry can be found in the text. An italic *m* indicates a map. Page references set in boldface type indicate the pages on which vocabulary terms are defined. Related entries are cross-referenced with *See* or *See also*. Guide words at the top of the pages help you identify which words appear on which page.

INDEX

INDEX

Seven hills of
ancient Rome,
*m*57

trade routes, *m*108

United States, I4–5

using, 184–185

Virginia, *m*184,
*m*188–189

voyages, *m*122–123,
*m*136, *m*142, *m*148,
*m*153

world, *m*I2, *m*I3,
*m*170–171,
*m*178–179

Marshall, Thurgood,
218, 238–239

Mecca, 105

Mediterranean Sea,
7–8, 9, 101

Memorial Day,
247, 249

Mexican Americans,
244–245

Migrant workers,
244–245

Military, 247–249, 255

Miners, 101

Mines, 97, 101, 108

Modify, 192, 193

Montreal, 148

Mosaics, 30, 69

Mosque, 113

Motivations, 131, 159

Mount Olympus, 13

Mountain ranges, 46,
52

Mountains, I6, 13,
16–17

Musical instruments,
103

Musicians, 103

Muslim, 105, 111, 113

Myths, 131, 141

N

National government,
225

National holidays,
249, 249–251. *See
also* Holidays

Natural resources, 6,
21

effect of goods and
services, 199

in Greece, 21

in Rome, 57, 63

raw materials and,
152

shipbuilding and,
63

uses of, 192

in West Africa, 93,
97, 101, 108

"New World," 137

Newport, Christopher,
125, 151, 152–155, 159

Niani, 109

Niger River, 91, 93, 96

Nobel Peace Prize, 243

Northern Hemisphere,
I3, 180

Northern Virginia, 176

Northwest Passage,
146

O

Oasis, 92

Oceans, I2

Atlantic, 8, 91,
130–131

Earth's, I2, 179

Olympic Games, 5,
32, 33

Opportunity, 263

Opportunity cost, 174,
206, 206–207

P

Paintings, 30, 45, 69

Parks, Rosa, 218,
240–241

Parthenon, 1, 3, 27,
28–29

Patriotism, 264

Peninsula, I6, 12, 50,
53, 61, 62

Pens, 48

Pericles, 5, 31

Permanent, 153

Physical
characteristics, 12

ancient places, 191

examples of, 188

Greece, 12–13, 16–17

Rome, 52–53, 56–57

West Africa, 92–93

Pictures, 188

Pie graph. *See* Circle
graph

Pilgrimage, 105

Plain, I6

Plato, 17, 30

Ponce de León, Juan,
124, 139, 140–143, 159

Population, 46, 61, 176,
189

Preserve, 97

Presidential Medal of
Freedom, 245

Presidents

Bill Clinton, 245

Thomas Jefferson,
232–233

Lyndon Johnson,
239, 243

Abraham Lincoln,
234–235

George
Washington, 230,
231, 264

Woodrow Wilson,
248

Prime meridian, 174,
181

Principle, 226

Producers, 20, 21, 196,
197

Protection, 24, 56, 88,
255

Puerto Rico, 140

Pursuit, 226

Q

Québec, 148

R

Rapids, 148, 154

Raw materials, 152

Reading Social
Studies Skills

Categorize and
Classify, 47–48

Cause and Effect,
87–88

Compare and
Contrast, 127–128

Draw Conclusions,
175–176

Generalize, 221–222

Main Idea and
Details, 7–8

Regions, 52, 174, 179,
199

Representative
democracy, 46, 70, 72

Republic, 70, 70–71, 72

Republican form of
government, 220,
231

Responsibility, 201,
254

Revolution, 230

INDEX

INDEX

VIRGINIA HISTORY AND SOCIAL SCIENCE STANDARDS OF LEARNING

History

3.1 The student will explain how the contributions of ancient Greece and Rome have influenced the present in terms of architecture, government (direct and representative democracy), and sports.

3.2 The student will study the early West African empire of Mali by describing its oral tradition (storytelling), government (kings), and economic development (trade).

3.3 The student will study the exploration of the Americas by

a) describing the accomplishments of Christopher Columbus, Juan Ponce de León, Jacques Cartier, and Christopher Newport;

b) identifying reasons for exploring, the information gained, the results of the travels, and the impact of these travels on American Indians.

Geography

3.4 The student will develop map skills by

a) locating Greece, Rome, and West Africa;

b) describing the physical and human characteristics of Greece, Rome, and West Africa;

c) explaining how the people of Greece, Rome, and West Africa adapted to and/or changed their environment to meet their needs.

3.5 The student will develop map skills by

a) positioning and labeling the seven continents and five oceans to create a world map;

b) using the equator and prime meridian to identify the Northern, Southern, Eastern, and Western Hemispheres;

c) locating the countries of Spain, England, and France;

d) locating the regions in the Americas explored by Christopher Columbus (San Salvador in the Bahamas), Juan Ponce de León (near St. Augustine, Florida), Jacques Cartier (near Québec, Canada), and Christopher Newport (Jamestown, Virginia);

e) locating specific places using a simple letter-number grid system.

3.6 The student will read and construct maps, tables, graphs, and/or charts.

Economics

3.7 The student will explain how producers in ancient Greece, Rome, and the West African empire of Mali used natural resources, human resources, and capital resources in the production of goods and services.

3.8 The student will recognize that because people and regions cannot produce everything they want, they specialize in producing some things and trade for the rest.

3.9 The student will identify examples of making an economic choice and will explain the idea of opportunity cost (what is given up when making a choice).

Civics

3.10 The student will recognize the importance of government in the community, Virginia, and the United States of America by

a) explaining the purpose of rules and laws;

b) explaining that the basic purposes of government are to make laws, carry out laws, and decide if laws have been broken;

c) explaining that government protects the rights and property of individuals.

3.11 The student will explain the importance of the basic principles that form the foundation of a republican form of government by

a) describing the individual rights to life, liberty, and the pursuit of happiness; and equality under the law;

b) identifying the contributions of George Washington, Thomas Jefferson, Abraham Lincoln, Rosa Parks, Thurgood Marshall, Martin Luther King, Jr., and César Chávez;

c) recognizing that Veterans Day and Memorial Day honor people who have served to protect the country's freedoms;

d) describing how people can serve the community, state, and nation.

3.12 The student will recognize that Americans are a people of diverse ethnic origins, customs, and traditions, who are united by the basic principles of a republican form of government and respect for individual rights and freedoms.